CLAIM YOUR
CONFIDENCE

Also by Lydia Fenet

The Most Powerful Woman in the Room Is You

CLAIM YOUR
CONFIDENCE

Unlock Your Superpower and Create the Life You Want

Lydia Fenet

Gallery Books

New York   London   Toronto   Sydney   New Delhi

G

Gallery Books
An Imprint of Simon & Schuster, Inc.
1230 Avenue of the Americas
New York, NY 10020

Copyright © 2023 by Lydia Fenet

First Gallery Books hardcover edition March 2023

GALLERY BOOKS and colophon are registered trademarks of Simon & Schuster, Inc.

For information about special discounts for bulk purchases,
please contact Simon & Schuster Special Sales at 1-866-506-1949
or business@simonandschuster.com.

The Simon & Schuster Speakers Bureau can bring authors to your live event.
For more information or to book an event, contact the Simon & Schuster Speakers Bureau at 1-866-248-3049 or visit our website at www.simonspeakers.com.

Interior design by Davina Mock-Maniscalco

Manufactured in the United States of America

10   9   8   7   6   5   4   3   2   1

Library of Congress Cataloging-in-Publication Data has been applied for.

ISBN 978-1-9821-9668-4
ISBN 978-1-9821-9670-7 (ebook)

Mom and Dad
Life is an adventure or nothing at all.
Thank you for giving me the love to support
such an extraordinary adventure.

———————

Chris
This has been a year with the highest highs and the lowest lows.
The one constant is my love for you.

———————

Beatrice, Henry, and Eloise
My brave, strong, beautiful children.
You are my everything. I love you so much.

———————

Charles, Andrew, and Hilary
Thank you for watching out for me, watching over me,
and trying to keep my feet on the ground.
You are the best siblings in the world.

CONTENTS

INTRODUCTION

CLAIM YOUR CONFIDENCE

Want to know a secret? You already have everything it takes to be confident. Every single thing you need is already inside you. It's time for you to claim that confidence and believe you have what it takes to live life on your terms. A life in which you value your own opinions over those around you. A life you live for you and no one else. The life that you deserve.

Today is the day you begin to build up your resilience, positivity, and fortitude and prepare yourself for that life, confident you are ready for anything that comes your way.

Maybe there was a time when you felt more confident than you do now. You could stride into a room or try something new without fear of being wrong. But these have been unusual times and difficult years, and somewhere in the ups and downs of life you may have forgotten what it feels like to be confident. Your confidence might be buried so deep you stopped listening to your own voice. Instead, you find yourself seeking answers from others, asking people what you should do with your life, and listening as if you haven't had the answers all along.

Maybe you've listened to other people for so long you don't remember you are the only one whose opinion matters. Or maybe you need someone to hold a mirror in front of you that reflects what deep down you already know: You have what it takes to walk into any room and believe that you are meant to be there. No matter your age—young, old, or somewhere in between—you still have time to grow, evolve, and act every single day to make sure that you are never in a place where others are in control of the narrative of your story.

That's not to say that claiming your confidence is easy. There may be challenges along the way that blindside you and shake you to the core. And over the course of your life, there will be unforeseen events that might make you feel like the entire world is against you. But the lessons you learn in this book will prepare you for those moments and give you the road map you need to stay strong. When the unexpected happens, when you are challenged in a way that makes you feel like you can't go on, you will have built layer upon layer of resilience during the times when the stakes are low so that you have the strength to overcome even the most difficult times.

When life is uncomfortable or hard, when you are scared and want to run from an experience, moving through it and trusting yourself will change you and make you believe in yourself. Everything you live through prepares you to handle something bigger, to become more resilient. If you have claimed your confidence and believe in yourself, you will be fine no matter what happens. And in many cases, you will come back stronger.

How do I know? Because I have spent the last twenty years of my life standing onstage as an auctioneer in front of thousands of people raising money for nonprofits around the world. It has taught me to push myself out of my comfort zone time and time again, to face my fears head-on, get comfortable with the uncomfortable, and shed my imposter syndrome. Each time my confidence was challenged, I learned to dig deeper and trust that I was strong enough to handle it, even when I feared I couldn't. Most importantly, it taught me to never give up, but to pivot and try again. And because of this, when I was tested in a way that I could have never foreseen, I was able to come back even stronger than before. This is what I want for you.

You thought you were opening this book to find a secret recipe for confidence. The secret is that there is no secret. You already have what it takes to be confident, but you have to believe it, too. It's time to close the door on your fears, insecurities, and everything that holds you back. It doesn't matter if you want to be the CEO of a company, the CEO of your family, or the CEO of a dream that only you can see. You will own every part of your story and live the life that you want.

This is your life, and your life story to write.

It's time to go all in.

Claim your confidence. It's time to go after the life you want.

1

THE TEFLON SHIELD

The bump of the wheels hitting the runway jolted me awake. Touch down San Francisco. April 2019. Two weeks after the launch of my first book, *The Most Powerful Woman in the Room Is You*.

As we taxied to the jet bridge, I reflected on the craziness of the past few weeks. They had been, in a word, a blur. The days and nights ran together into a never-ending loop as I juggled time with the kids, my job, and book signings. The pace had been dizzying, but the exhilaration outweighed the exhaustion.

Two weeks prior, on a beautiful April evening, I had sat along-side my family, friends, and colleagues at a dinner celebrating the launch of my book. I felt like I was living in a dream as I looked out at the iconic Rockefeller Center building across the street. The ride home from my book party felt like the most New York moment of all New York moments, and the words of Frank Sinatra floated through my head: *"If I can make it there, I'll make it anywhere . . ."* This was my "made it" moment.

Now, as I got off the plane, I could feel the adrenaline coursing through my veins. I was buzzing with excitement as if I had finished three cups of coffee instead of just waking up from a cat nap. I pulled my bag out of the overhead compartment on the plane and walked quickly through the airport, excited to be in one of my favorite cities and for the events of the next few days. As I passed a Hudson News bookseller, a flash of hot pink caught my eye. *The Most Powerful Woman in the Room Is You* was prominently displayed next to the cash register. *My book! In the wild! In a major international airport!* I couldn't believe it. How many times had I walked by newsstands in airports around the world and paused to peruse the books section?

I rushed over to the cashier and excitedly told him that it was my book on the counter next to him. He couldn't have been nicer—he immediately told all the women working in the store that it was my book, and each of them posed for pictures with me. He even let me sign the copies next to the register. I stood in the back of the store for a few minutes waiting to see if anyone purchased one, but everyone seemed to be going in and out so quickly they barely gave it a glance. In a sales situation like this you have two choices:

1. You can feel dismayed that no one is picking up your book or whatever you have created,

or—and this I highly recommend—

2. See it as a challenge. A room full of sales potential. Remember that no one will ever sell something that you created as well as you. If it is yours, take every single opportunity to promote, sell, and tell everyone about it. Lose the embarrassment. You created it. You need to tell everyone why they should buy it.

Never one to miss an opportunity to sell anything, I announced loudly to everyone in the store that I was the author of the book on the counter and would be happy to personalize it if anyone needed a gift. An older gentleman who was purchasing a bottle of water bought a copy for his granddaughter. I told him he should read it too. I couldn't contain my excitement. One more sale than I had when I walked into the store. Watch out, Danielle Steel!

San Francisco was the second leg of my book tour after New York, and I wanted to bring as much energy to the West Coast as I had to the East Coast. I was in town for three days, eager to take advantage of every offer to talk about my book. A couple of months before the book was published, I emailed everyone who offered to host something, along with anyone I knew in San Francisco. The email was short: Could anyone connect me with an opportunity to speak about the book in a large setting? By the time I finished my emails, I had plenty lined up: from an event at Twitter to a cocktail party to a book signing at the Ferry Building in downtown San Francisco.

I arrived at my friend Auburn's house, my home away from home when I travel to the West Coast, to have a moment of downtime. The next morning was the first official stop of my San Francisco book tour; I'd have a moderated talk at a local bookstore in San Francisco with a local radio personality who happened to moonlight as a charity auctioneer. After that wrapped up, I would head to a cocktail party and book signing followed by an intimate dinner at a nearby restaurant. I had invited all my San Francisco friends to the evening event since the New York book signing events at bookstores had done well on bookstore promotion alone. It never occurred to me that I needed to invite people to the bookstore event in the middle of the day. Never one to shy away from a crowd, and always assuming a positive outcome, I just knew it would be a sold-out event. Full disclosure: my unwavering optimism helps me always see the good in any situation, but it sometimes blinds me to the good advice of others who have gone before me.

I shot out of bed early the next morning, still on East Coast time, and decided to use the extra hours to go for a run. Running has always been a necessity for me whenever traveling in and out of time zones simply because it helps me get over jet lag quickly and clears my head. By the time I returned to Auburn's house, made a dent in my emails, and took a shower, Auburn's family was up. We chatted excitedly about the upcoming day as Auburn quickly gave me a makeover. She's a lawyer by trade but has secretly always wanted to be a makeup artist. As a result, I always walk out of her house looking like I've spent an hour with a Glamsquad team.

Feeling great despite the early wake up that morning, I slid into the Uber ready to take on the day. As I sat in traffic on the way to the book event, my thoughts were on the cocktail party and dinner that evening. I couldn't have been more excited to see everyone and share my book on the West Coast. I could already imagine a packed event and a line of friends waiting to have their books signed. I stared out of the window at the beautiful blue sky, watching as the Golden Gate Bridge came into view at the top of one of the hills. It all felt so perfect. So very, very perfect.

Feeling a little tired of all the perky perfection? Don't worry— this story is about to take a real U-turn.

As we drove to the Ferry Building in downtown San Francisco, Waze showed traffic building up ahead. I had left plenty of time, but as the arrival time on the app kept getting later and later, I started to feel nervous that we were going to miss the book signing. By the time we arrived only twelve minutes before the book talk started, I was frantic, practically knocking over people as I sprinted to the bookstore trying not to trip in heels. I rounded the corner to the bookstore with ten minutes to spare, pausing outside the door to catch my breath so that I didn't look as frazzled as I felt. A trick for any situation where you feel everything is out of control: pause. Take a deep breath, exhale, take another deep breath, put your shoulders back, and put the biggest smile you can muster on your face. No one else knows how you are feeling on the inside. As long as you appear to be in control, people will assume you have it all together. Even the most confident person will tell you, sometimes you have to fake it until you make it. Or fake it until you feel like you've made it. And remember, no one knows that you are faking it except for you. Through the window I could see rows of chairs set up in a semi-circle. The charity auctioneer/radio host was seated in one chair holding a microphone, but other than that, the chairs were empty.

Well, not entirely empty. There was one young woman seated in the second row.

I glanced at my phone again. Nine minutes to go. Where were all the people? I had a sick feeling that I was in the wrong place, but that couldn't be . . . The host was clearly there. Maybe I had the wrong time? Perhaps my clock was stuck on East Coast time? I checked my phone.

No. It was 12:21 PST. I was right on time.

One look at the warm, slightly embarrassed smile of the local bookstore owner holding my book gave me the answer. No one was coming.

All of a sudden, I had a fleeting memory of a conversation with another author about her book tour. Over dinner one night she was recounting one of her first book signings where only a handful of people showed up. She hated public speaking and told me, "I don't know which is worse at a book signing—no one showing up and you just leave, or one person showing and then you still have to hold the talk." In that moment I decided, *one person*. The answer is definitely one person, because you still have to give the talk. As I stood staring at the empty room, I realized that my dream of a packed crowd was exactly that, a dream.

I was absolutely mortified. I felt absurd standing there in full makeup with my hair blown out, evidence that I thought that it was going to be a sold-out event. Putting in all that effort now made me feel ridiculous; it belied how important I thought this event was going to be—my misguided belief that I could have a successful event just by showing up. I had expected this to be something big, when it wasn't even going to be small. It was going to be a book talk for one person. I walked in and grinned sheepishly and said as much to the bookstore owner.

She gave me a half smile back and said, "Maybe we should start a few minutes late." The charity auctioneer with whom I was supposed to be in conversation remained seated at the front of the room. Our eyes met, and he shrugged his shoulders with a kind smile. I felt an immediate bond with him. As a charity auctioneer you are used to being in front of crowds of people who never pay attention. It takes a strong constitution to stand in front of hundreds of people, trying to raise money, while they do their best to drown out your voice. I knew if I could commiserate with anyone, it would be him.

A minute passed before I heard the door open again. The bookstore owner and I turned at the same time, staring hopefully at the door as if willing a last-minute rush of people.

A woman my age walked straight up to us. *Finally*, I thought.

"Hi! I'm looking for a gluten-free cookbook."

God, please make it stop, I thought.

"Um—I'm not sure—maybe over there?" pointed the owner. The woman walked quickly away from us, barely glancing at the empty seats that took over half of the store.

I heard the door open again. I turned expectantly, ever hopeful. In walked one of my little sister's best friends.

I felt my face flush with embarrassment. "And now there is a witness to the fact that this is a total disaster."

I should pause here to tell you that my sister is the funniest person I know. She uses that sense of humor to keep me in check by making fun of me at every opportunity. No matter how bad something is, calling and telling her about it immediately makes it better because she always makes light of it. I can't overstate the importance of humor when things are going wrong. It is a tool I use onstage constantly—the worse the moment, the bigger the joke. I could already hear the peals of laughter as I told her that I was holding a book talk for two people. I would never live this down.

Her friend looked at the empty chairs quizzically and walked over to me. "Did I get the time wrong?" she said as she gave me a hug.

"Nope. I decided to hold a book talk for just you, but unfortunately, someone else showed up."

She laughed. "Oh no. I am so sorry."

In a worst-case scenario, this felt pretty worst case.

———

Are you squirming in your seat right now? Feeling pity but possibly a little happy that after so much positivity there was something that didn't feel quite as glossy? (It's okay, we're all human.)

I want you to close your eyes and imagine this is your moment instead of mine. Go ahead and really sit with this uncomfortable feeling. The truth is, this feeling, this fear of embarrassment has kept me from doing so many things in life. Imagine this moment: a highly publicized event, one that you have shared on social media, hyped up for everyone to see, the expectation that this would be a sold-out crowd, and then only two people show up. Think of all the feelings that accompany a moment like this—humiliation, rejection, shame—feelings that prevent you from going after things because you are scared that you won't succeed. That you might offer up a product or service that nobody thinks is good enough. That you are standing on the precipice of a goal or a dream and someone will tell you that you can't do it, or that you aren't good enough. That you will say or do something that people will think is stupid or make fun of you for after you leave a room because they feel it is too forward, or, as the kids say, "extra." Feel all of this. All the feelings.

Here's the hard truth: *This* is where confidence is born. *This* is where you earn your stripes, where you realize that you can overcome all the things and feelings that threaten to stop you.

If you are going to claim your confidence, this will be a part of your journey. You have to put yourself in situations where you are putting yourself out there, and where failure is a very real possibility. There will be highs, there will be lows, and there will be many times that are somewhere in between. You might think that these challenging moments are ones to forget. But actually, you need to flip the script. *These* are the moments that make the journey worth it. *These* are the moments that ground us, center us, and remind us that no matter how great everything is in your life—life will always have a way of reminding you that you are human.

Confidence comes from understanding this and pushing forward in spite of the fact that something like this could happen to you. Because when you claim your confidence, no matter how embarrassed you are at that moment, no matter how badly you feel about yourself, you will live to tell the story and grow stronger because you met the moment.

Confidence means understanding that even if something doesn't go your way, even if that something you desperately want isn't happening, you won't turn and run. You will face it head-on.

It's not what happens to you that makes you successful or unsuccessful. It's how you handle it, and how you tell the story to put yourself back in control.

And since you have been sitting with this mortifying experience for long enough, let me take you through what you need to know in order to handle a worst-case scenario moment.

I describe the "Strike Method" in *The Most Powerful Woman in the Room Is You,* a signature move to help ground you when entering any situation. Well, just like you need to have one to own your power, you need to make sure you have another one in your arsenal to help you display the utmost confidence, no matter what those around you might think.

At the end of my very first book tour event, a woman stood up at the end of the Q & A. She said, "I don't have any questions, but I did want to tell you that I worked at a call center where I was rejected over ten thousand times. I tell people I am made of Teflon. Rejection just bounces off me." I never forgot that, and I adopted it into my own confidence arsenal.

So the first tool for when you are in a situation where you feel your least confident is to mentally put up that Teflon shield. Not just in front of you, put it around and over your entire body, so that you are completely protected. Other people's thoughts, comments, dislike of who you are and what you are doing do not touch you.

Confidence comes from within. Power comes from within. All of that stays within that shield, and everything else bounces off you.

Project your most confident "you," rather than projecting anxiety about negative thoughts relating to what you imagine people may be thinking of you. Side note: most likely those people aren't thinking those negative things about you anyway, so it's a waste of your precious time to worry about it!

Second, be the superpower in your own life story. *You* shape the narrative of your life. *You* write your life story with your words and your actions. You can choose to unleash your superpower, your confidence, in any situation. You know the people in your life who can never see the good in anything? The person who always presents a story with a negative spin about how they didn't get what they wanted because of something or someone else? How things are always happening *to* them? Stop right there. That is not you. Think about how you want the story to turn out and what you can control in that moment and *do it*. In that bookstore at that moment, I could not control the number of people who sat in the seats for the book signing, right? Or could I?

Which brings me to the final thing to remember. You need to find your angle. How are you going to turn a situation, a conversation, or something that is going terribly awry into something positive?

Let's rewrite the ending to this story, shall we?

After years spent onstage at charity auctions dying on the inside when everything is going badly—no one raising their hand to bid, the crowd speaking so loudly that I can't even hear myself speak, or a waiter tipping a tray of glassware onto the floor and activating an entire cleanup crew right in front of me as an audience looks on—

I've learned that you can summon confidence even in the most challenging moments.

Back in that nearly empty bookstore in San Francisco, I took a deep breath, pulled my shoulders back, and put a smile on my face. Then I said to myself, *Let's work with what we've got.*

I looked around. There were two women in the store, in addition to the woman who was looking for cookbooks. I knew the owner of the store would take a seat. *Well, four people is better than two!*

I walked up to the woman who had asked about the gluten-free cookbook. "Hi! I'm Lydia Fenet. I'm giving a book talk in five minutes about my new book, *The Most Powerful Woman in the Room Is You.* I'd love it if you could join—it will be about half an hour." I showed her the book cover and smiled.

She looked at me, looked at the empty chairs, and then looked back at me again. She glanced down at the book in my outstretched hands.

"No thanks," she said, and she turned back to the stacks.

I almost laughed out loud. *Seriously? Not even out of pity? Teflon shield, Lydia. Let that comment bounce off you and keep going,* I thought.

Cardinal rule of sales—it isn't personal, it's business. On to the next.

I approached the other two women in the store and asked them the same thing. Whether they were interested in the book or simply took pity on me, they agreed to join me for the talk and took their seats. *Great!* I thought. Three guests, my sister's friend, plus the bookstore owner makes five. *Quite a crowd! What a selling star!* It wasn't great, but it made me feel better to know that I would have at least one book sale, even if I bought the book and gifted it to my sister's friend.

At 12:40 it was pretty clear that we had all the guests we were going to have for this talk. I moved back over to the chair to take my seat, and I realized that someone else had joined the audience while I was trying to convince people to join me. In the back of the room, another woman had taken a seat in the back row. Based on the fact that she had pulled a small shopping cart that held a suitcase, a bag filled with plastic bottles, and a huge pile of cardboard, I'd assumed she was homeless. The owner of the store noticed as well and came over to me and whispered, "She comes in and listens to the talks sometimes. I feel badly asking her to leave. She might be a little disruptive, but she means well. Do you want me to ask her to leave?"

I shook my head. First of all, I was thrilled that we would have six people. Moreover, disruptive is something I can handle. Standing onstage as a charity auctioneer, I am used to people yelling out bids, guests who have been overserved, people climbing onstage "just to say something for a minute."

"No, it's fine!"

Not a minute after the radio host asked me the first question, the woman at the back of the room started interrupting with comments in a loud voice. At first, I tried to talk over her in an effort to answer questions directly, but as I saw the other guests squirming in their chairs every time she piped up, I realized that I needed to stop talking over her and bring her into the conversation. Why try to pretend something isn't happening when every single person sitting in the room is watching the same thing? Remember, you control the narrative, you control the story, so do not be the losing character in your story. Once again, I found myself feeling thankful for all those nights onstage when things went wrong, when the noise from the audience threatened to completely overpower my voice, and I learned that instead of running offstage I had to dig deep and find a way to make it work.

The next time she made a comment, I immediately incorporated it into the conversation. Interestingly, since the interviewer was a charity auctioneer, he was used to playing to the crowd—and he immediately understood what I was doing and started doing it too. Was it the best book talk I have ever given? Definitely not. Was it the best book talk where I was speaking to five people when it was supposed to be forty? Definitely. And did I live to tell the story? Yes.

After a half hour talking about the book and incorporating additional thoughts from our heckler into the speech, the interviewer looked out into the crowd.

"Does anyone have any questions?"

I was pretty sure I knew the answer.

Our new friend in the back raised her hand. "I think the next time you do this it should be a potluck."

I smiled. "That's a good idea. When we hold auctions we always feed everyone so that they stay longer." I laughed a little. "Well, that and an open bar."

She looked at me seriously. "No. You have to stay away from booze. That's how I ended up on the street."

And . . . scene.

That night, I walked into a packed crowd at my friend's store, Hero Shop. It was everything I had hoped it would be and more. I spent the entire night signing books, connecting with women who wanted to know more about the book, and seeing friends who had shown up to support me.

After the book signing ended, a woman who had worked on my team at Christie's years prior and had since become one of my closest friends put together a small group for dinner. As I finally had the chance to relax and enjoy a glass of wine, the questions about the book tour came fast and furious. *How was the dinner at Christie's? You are going on the* Today *show? How was the talk at CBS? Twitter? Google?*

Did you ever expect it to be like this?

I thought about the question for a minute. The truth is, my Instagram feed was filled with perfect pictures from the two weeks prior. I had only snapped one shot for my Instagram Story showing the earlier book talk, and I didn't exactly snap the empty seats. I thought about the message of my book, about the importance of honesty in selling and telling your story.

"Well, if you must know . . . the biggest success was the book signing this morning." Then I explained what happened. In much the same way I just told you this story, I led them to believe that I anticipated it would be a wild success . . . and then gave them every granular detail about the mortification of a six-person book talk. By the end we were all laughing until tears streamed down our faces.

We may only want success, but it's the moments that really knock the wind out of you that show you what you're made of. Confidence doesn't mean perfect. Confidence means that you are secure in who you are and what you are doing regardless of what is happening in your life. Confidence is being able to laugh at yourself among people you admire, knowing that they admire you even more for it because they realize you aren't afraid of getting knocked down. Because the truth is in life, you will get knocked down, but you will get up again and be stronger for the lesson you have learned. You might have a few more bruises and bumps, but you will come out stronger for realizing you were able to get through it.

Are you ready to claim your confidence? Because once you claim it there is no turning back. The good and bad will come in equal measure in your life. There will be moments when you are striding confidently down the streets of New York City believing that Frank Sinatra wrote the lyrics to "New York, New York" for you and you alone, and the next moment you will be at an empty book event begging people to attend. Quite often those two things come as a package deal. What matters is that you experience those highs and lows and learn from them. Don't allow these moments to diminish your confidence—let them make you realize that confidence doesn't come from crowd size, Instagram likes, or press accolades. It comes from knowing that no matter what happens in your life, you have the ability to handle it.

You ready? It's time to claim your confidence and go after the life you want.

ASHLEY BAKER STAATS

Deputy Editor at Air Mail and
Co-Host of *Morning Meeting* podcast

I had no business becoming a handbag designer—I'm a trained journalist—but in my late twenties, I went ahead and did it anyway. It was a project I embarked upon with a childhood friend, and we threw ourselves into this notoriously challenging ecosystem with a lot of passion and drive. After about two years of moderate success and massive time investment, we closed the business; it would never be the financial unicorn that we had hoped. But a decade later, it's so clear that this particular failure set the stage for so many successes. Not only did I learn the intricacies of running the back end of a business—something I had never encountered in my day job—but it also became something of a graduate study course in business administration.

Ultimately, I returned to journalism, and I have brought that entrepreneurial ethos to every organization I've worked at. And perhaps most importantly, I developed a much clearer understanding of my strengths and weaknesses. Despite the challenges of the business, my cofounder and I remain close friends—which, for me, is the ultimate success.

2

NEVER GIVE UP

If you listen to the way most people talk about success in life, success is a mountain that you climb, and one day you will reach the top of your personal Mount Everest. If money is your motivation, it's the day that you hit a certain dollar amount in your bank account and have so much cash in the bank that you can simply throw dollar bills in the air fist pumping. If you are an athlete, it's the day you stand atop the Olympic podium with a gold medal. Or, if fame is your thing, it's the day you stand onstage at the Academy Awards choking back tears as you clutch the Oscar to the bodice of your couture gown. Whatever success looks like to you, there is probably an image of what the pinnacle looks like that you have been envisioning throughout your adult life. Yet, ask anyone who you believe has reached the zenith of their mountain and they will tell you, what you reach is not the top of the mountain, it's just the beginning of another climb.

I have always been in love with words. As a child I spent far too many nights reading a book at night by the crack of light shining from my closet door instead of sleeping. I was always fascinated by language and the way words on a page could transport me to a different continent or world. There is something magical about the fact that a single word can describe an entire movement or moment, and over the course of my life there are certain words that have stuck with me from the minute I read or heard them and stayed with me forever.

One of those moments came in high school right before one of the toughest lacrosse games of the season. As we sat on the sidelines waiting for the referee to whistle, signaling the start of the game, our coach gave us a pep talk: "You ladies need heart to win this game, but most of all, you need tenacity." I saw a few of the other girls looking around, unsure whether we should interrupt this "We Are the Champions" speech. One girl next to me raised her hand. "What does 'tenacity' mean?" Our coach looked at us, eyes filled with intensity. "It's the quality possessed by a person who sticks with a goal even when things aren't going her way. It's someone who commits and keeps trying, no matter what." Well, I thought, maybe in SAT language the word is "tenacity," but in my family it's a simple phrase: never give up.

"Never give up" was not just a phrase in our house; it was the most important phrase in our house. It's a phrase that has motivated me throughout my life when things are good, but more important, when things are bad. It reminds me time and time again that it's not always about winning, but rather being confident enough in yourself to keep trying even when the odds are stacked against you. It em-

boldens you to believe that if the goal is there, you keep
matter the outcome. It isn't always about hitting that goal, b
the lessons learned from the journey to get there. I should
learned one of the greatest lessons about never giving up in
school.

I am one of four kids—two boys, two girls—all taller t
average kid, with parents who were enthusiastic in their
even if we were mediocre, because for them, trying was
portant part, not winning. That philosophy served us well,
would all try out for everything and anything no matter our
ability.

My father played football in high school, and he assum
sons would do the same, but his British wife would have or
when her first son was born: no football. My dad, never
shy away from an opportunity to try something new, decided
couldn't have a son who played football, he might as well st
own soccer team. Go big or go home, right? And if your name i
and you start a team, there is really only one name for your
the Bobcats. Since my older brother and I were only twenty m
apart, it meant that I became an unwilling participant in the w
soccer practices coached by my dad, as well as a member of tl
lustrious team comprised of first and second graders. Each we
we huddled together in the blistering Louisiana heat, listenir
whatever pearls of wisdom my dad would dispense about the t
that we were about to play, the final few moments of the hu
were always the same. We would stack our little hands on to
each other in the circle and my dad would shout, "What's the Bok

rule?" Our little voices would mingle together as we shouted back, "NEVER GIVE UP!"

As the Bobcats continued their domination of the youth soccer league in Louisiana, my parents mercifully decided that I could give up soccer. But that wasn't the end of my athletic career by any stretch of the imagination; I continued playing myriad sports. The small school that I attended had a graduating class of—drum roll, please—twelve students. Let's just say that our sports teams weren't exactly crushing the competition on any given day.

By the time I reached sixth grade I was playing volleyball, basketball, and running track for my school. How I loved playing on the sports teams in middle school. The camaraderie, the team spirit, the cute uniforms, the orange slices at halftime, the pep rallies—the *Friday Night Lights* feel of playing competitive sports in a small southern town. Truly it was everything that you could want in a small-town athletic experience. The only thing that was missing? A winning team.

That's right. In *four* years of playing for *three* different sports teams, we never won a game.

By never won a game, I mean that we were never even *close* to winning a game. We would lose basketball games 52–6 or 44–2. Unlike in school sports today, there was no mercy shown from the opposing teams. No one cared if the other team was running up the score. We would play schools where they had fifty kids in the eighth-grade class and they would absolutely crush us, in every sport, time and time again. There was one game when the score was so high, they told the other team not to raise their hands in defense.

Didn't matter; none of us could really shoot the ball, so the score was still double digits to single digits. We lost, and we lost big.

Week after week, year after year, you would think all of that losing would really have crushed the spirit of a group of middle schoolers. But the amazing thing was that we all believed, no matter how badly we had been beaten time and time again, there was a chance we would win the next game. Each week we would get dressed in our uniforms, tie ribbons in our hair, apply a little lip gloss when our moms weren't looking, and cheer on our teammates like we were going for Olympic gold. This cheering was usually taking place from the court, because when you only have six players on the team, there isn't a lot of "bench time." But if you had taken a poll right before any of the games in those three years, I assure you I would have told you we were going to win. This story doesn't have a happy ending like you would expect. There was never a moment where we came from behind to win a big game like you see in the movies.

After each and every game, I would walk over to the bleachers where my parents sat cheering me on every game. As a parent, I now understand that part of your role as a parent is letting your children figure things out on their own, to fail no matter how painful it is for you to watch, and to not give away the end of the story even when you are fairly certain of the outcome. So at the end of every game, instead of telling me I could do better or indulging my sadness or, perhaps, saying less than flattering things about the other team, they would say something more along the lines of "That was a really tough loss. They were a really good team." I would nod, completely deflated and, truth be told, shocked that we had lost yet again. And then, without missing a beat they would say, "I think the next game is going to be the one you win." All of a sudden that sadness turned into a smile, and I would nod my head excitedly, already thinking about the glory and excitement of the win the next week. "Me too," I would reply.

Although you were probably reading the above paragraph wincing at the thought of a four-year losing streak, or how many times my parents had to sit through a game where they knew the ending before the first whistle was blown or, perhaps, feeling sorry for a group of middle school girls who were trounced on a weekly basis, you shouldn't waste your pity on me. I truly believe that losing streak was one of the most formative experiences of my life. Losing so many times, yet knowing that we had to go back out there a week later and try it all over again, taught me an even greater lesson: what it means to truly never give up no matter the odds, no matter what you are up against. It gave me the foundation for the confidence I have needed my whole life to keep reaching for new goals even when all the odds seemed stacked against me. My delusional optimism likely started years ago when I was walking onto a court knowing that we had lost the prior game 52–2 but still believing that we had a shot at actually winning the next game. In both my personal and professional life, I have come to understand the importance of never giving up, even when you are unsure of the outcome. When you commit to this philosophy in life, you will quickly notice that by making this phrase your personal mantra, you are in a class by yourself. Most people are quick to self-select anytime something challenges them or pushes them out of their comfort zone. By staying in the race and continuing to try even when things aren't going your way, you will learn how to accept it even when things don't go your way. Because in life, sometimes things won't work out, sometimes they will, but you will also understand the most important lesson of all: you'll never succeed if you give up. The next time you feel like opting out or throwing up your hands and walking away from what seems like an impossible situation, remember that if you keep trying, sometimes it will all reveal itself in the end.

People who have climbed the mountain and reached the pinnacle of success realize that they didn't reach the zenith, they simply reached a plateau that gives them a runway to find their next mountain to climb. Life becomes more interesting when you are happy to throw paint against the wall until something sticks. But the other part about not giving up is that you always have to be ready to pivot. Never giving up doesn't mean that you have to run into a brick wall over and over again. At times you will need to change the direction of your efforts, to ensure that you can keep moving forward. Nothing is gained from never giving up and not realizing that something isn't working. Unlike sports teams in middle school where you have a finite number of players and talent, in real life opportunities abound for those willing to take risks and try new things. Don't get stuck in one lane trying the same thing over and over again. Be open to feedback, to criticism, to ideas, but most of all to people who offer to help. When I see someone who shows persistence and tenacity, I am always willing to extend a hand or make an introduction because I know that it won't be wasted. There is nothing worse than referring someone who never takes advantage of the opportunity. Be the person who chooses to make the most of any opportunity put in front of them even if it doesn't go the way you thought it would. Remember that even in moments when it seems like there is no path forward, there is always a solution if you have the attitude that giving up isn't an option.

And then there are moments in life when you *think* you have reached the top of your personal mountain and when momentum seems to be going in your favor—but even in these moments you can be tested. The only thing that matters is that you don't give up. You find a solution; you make it work. You never give up.

By my late twenties, my life in New York had taken on a familiar cadence. During the day I worked ten to twelve hours a day running the events department at Christie's. Over the course of the year, my team and I barely had time to breathe, as we worked to ensure every event detail was covered while also planning and executing hundreds of events. But at night when the rest of the team was usually winding down their day job after the event ended at 8:00 p.m., the end of the event signaled something else for me: the beginning of my night shift.

In the final fifteen minutes of the event, as the waiters started to close down the bars and remove glasses that needed to be cleaned in anticipation of another event the next evening, I would dash upstairs to my office. Time for a quick change into a cocktail dress. I would throw my heels into a carrier bag and make sure my trusty purse-sized gavel and auction notes were tucked neatly into my purse. While the event guests were politely encouraged to move toward the front doors,

I was slipping out the back door applying lipstick or putting in a pair of sparkly earrings as I walked, to use my time efficiently. Every minute of my evening was precisely timed to ensure I had enough time for a quick debrief before I commanded the stage to raise money at a charity auction somewhere in the city. After the auction my night never ended when I left the auction stage. I almost always made plans to meet up with my friends wherever they were after the auctions. I would usually roll in just as they were finishing dessert. It was a demanding schedule, but I loved every second of it.

In the nonprofit world there are auctions and then there are AUCTIONS. One of my first experiences seeing the type of auction you write in all caps, and the type of auction that became the zenith of *my* personal mountain, took place during my first couple of years at Christie's. I was still firmly at the bottom of the special events department ladder, so I was no longer an intern but the coordinator of a department who had yet to try out to become an auctioneer. At the time, the special events team organized spotters to accompany our top auctioneers around the city, ensuring they always had extra backup during the big auctions. The spotters were typically young women who volunteered their evening to spot bidders in exchange for the opportunity to attend the nonprofit galas.

Well, "attend" might be a stretch; we weren't exactly mixing with the guests. Instead we would sit in the back eating the staff meal while the guests enjoyed cocktails during cocktail hour. Right before the auction, we would all move from backstage to the auction room where celebrities and New York society sat at tables enjoying the evening's entertainment and, hopefully, for the auctioneer's sake, a few glasses of wine. We would stand between the groups of tables yelling out "BIDDING!" if the auctioneer was missing a bidder's hand amid the controlled chaos of a thousand-person gala. Organizations used all sorts of methods to make sure the auctioneer could see us: glow sticks, whistles, oversized paddles with a huge logo on the front. Our main job was to ensure that the auctioneer always knew if there were people bidding, and to make sure that not one bid was lost, in an effort to raise money for a great cause.

For a group of young twenty-year-old women who wanted to see the glitz and glamour New York had to offer, it was a dream come true. Although we had assisted with many smaller auctions in my first couple of years in the company, there was one auction that was truly next-level in terms of its glitz and celebrity . . . and the number of dresses that people had procured in so many shades of pink. In addition to all the glamour, there was one reason that this event stuck out in particular: it was the first time I watched the auctioneer and knew exactly what I wanted to do.

Every year in New York City, the Breast Cancer Research Foundation hosts the Hot Pink Party for Breast Cancer Research. The nonprofit was founded by Evelyn Lauder and has raised millions of dollars to fund research to end breast cancer. Since its inception, the evening has been hosted by Elizabeth Hurley, with other celebrity friends making appearances throughout the night, culminating in a bring-down-the-house performance by Elton John. In today's fast-paced world, pictures from these events would be all over every social media site within seconds of a celebrity arrival à la Lady Gaga or the Kardashians at the Met Ball. But at that time, social media didn't exist, so only the best pictures made the coveted spots in *Vogue* and *Vanity Fair* a month after the event took place. It made the entire event feel completely exclusive and incredibly exciting to someone who had only read about these types of events up until that night.

Christie's had offered to send our auctioneer as well as a team of spotters to assist with the auction for the inaugural Hot Pink Party. As you can imagine, given the excitement around the event, there were plenty of women who had volunteered to join the bidding and spotting team. We had all changed into our black dresses and suits in the bathrooms at Christie's and walked from Rockefeller Center to Park Avenue, where the Waldorf stood with pink lights adorning the outside of the building in honor of the event. Judging from the paparazzi staking out the front door of the Waldorf, it was clear that we were about to the enter the type of event I had dreamed of since I started working at Christie's. As our group approached the red carpet, the paparazzi pivoted swiftly before they realized we weren't people whose pictures would result in a payday. They quickly turned back to look for guests who, at the very least, had followed the dress code instructions: THINK PINK!

We pushed through the revolving doors of the Waldorf Astoria, past women dressed from head to toe in pink and holding clipboards directing everyone to the event. As we passed by the room where cocktail hour was taking place, we took a quick peek and caught a glimpse of some celebrities mingling with over eight hundred New Yorkers dressed in various shades of hot pink. Although the auction was in the middle of the evening, we were allowed to stay to watch the performance as a thank-you for our time. The minute we walked out of the Waldorf I promptly called my parents to recount every single detail, including the final moment of Elton's performance, which he played in a fully sequined gold outfit. It was unforgettable on every level, but for me, the standout moment was during the auction. As I watched the auctioneer onstage, the crowd chattering loudly as he called out the bids, I remember thinking, *I want to be up on that stage. I want to be the auctioneer at this event.*

Well, it took ten years of late nights, hundreds and hundreds of auctions, long hours, and hard work before I had my chance. After passing the charity auctioneering class at Christie's in my early twenties, I took any auction that was offered. It became something of a joke with other auctioneers. Because I was so eager to take auctions, they knew that even if they decided to back out at the last minute, I had cocktail dresses on the back of my door and could run out at a moment's notice. But over the years, as I became more skilled as an auctioneer, the opportunities grew for bigger and more complex auctions. Without realizing it, my confidence in my ability to get on a stage, any stage, anywhere in the country and provide a performance at the highest level put me in the top echelon of auctioneers. Gone were the days that I had to beg to take auctions; the asks were now coming directly to me.

Yet there were a few auctions that were always taken by our senior auctioneers or top auctioneers from Sotheby's and Phillips. Because I was still young, and my belief in my abilities hadn't caught up with my actual abilities, I never felt comfortable suggesting myself for anything for fear of being rejected or given a pat on the head with a "This is for the grown-ups, Lydia," which was something a colleague had once said to me when I raised my hand for an auction. While I never pushed the issue, I knew that if I kept working hard enough, at some point I would be so good that they couldn't ignore me.

Ten years into my auctioneering career, with ten thousand hours fully under my belt, it happened. A board member of the Breast Cancer Research Foundation had seen me take an auction, and an email was sent from BCRF to our chairman asking if I could take the auction for the Hot Pink Party. I'm pretty sure you know the answer to that question.

The first thing that came to mind after running around my office jumping up and down with excitement was not auction related. It was "Where am I going to find something that is hot pink and worthy of being on a stage with Elton John??" "With" Elton John might be a bit of a stretch because we were never actually together onstage, but this was before the iPhone, so just indulge me for this story.

I believe networking at all levels is incredibly important through-out your life and career. As you grow in your career, the people you start out with in various industries become your early twenties life class. Some do well and excel, others leave the class and go some-where else, others finish but never do anything with what they learned. In my early years at Christie's, I took advantage of any invitation that was extended to me or to which one of the more senior women in the events department invited me. As a result, I had the opportunity to meet people in other industries. It was in these early years that I met a lot of young women my age in many different roles in various companies who are still close friends today.

While I was busy stuffing gift bags and checking people in at events at Christie's, I met plenty of women who were doing the equivalent in the fashion industry, i.e., wading through piles of samples while being yelled at by every celebrity assistant in the world to get clothes for their celebrity to wear on the red carpet. Since we had stuck together and commiserated in those sleepless, overworked/underpaid years of our life, we were all bonded on a level that meant that we were in it to win it: we knew what it meant to work hard, get our hands dirty, and support each other and each other's careers. In my case, any time I needed a dress or a gown to wear at an auction, I would send an email to my friends who, also a decade into their careers, were now PR managers at fashion houses in New York. They knew that as the auctioneer I would get photographed onstage by the photographers. But more important, they knew that I would hustle for them and could always be counted on to seek out a reporter or editor attending the event, to make sure that the name of the designer was mentioned along with any pictures they might use from the event. This meant my friends could show their boss that they were crushing their job by getting the word out about their collection, while I had the opportunity to borrow dresses I couldn't afford. Add to that, I wasn't demanding steep fees for wearing their dresses, like celebrities. I was just excited to have something different to wear each night instead of the clothes that weren't on par with what the guests of the event were wearing.

When you are at the bottom of the career ladder, know that the hustle is a large part of how you get to the next step. It is so easy in this day and age to look at someone's social media profile and believe that it was all so effortless. I assure you that no matter how effortless someone makes it look, there were many days and likely years before they made it to a place where it looked effortless. I can't tell you how many times I missed out on friends' birthday parties, trips, and events because I was taking an auction every single night of the week. I gave up a lot to pursue the path to success, but I wanted it. It was my goal, and when you set a goal that you want, you are the only person who can make it happen. Success takes hard work, ingenuity, and risk. It also takes asking for things that might help you in your path, even if you are squirming as you make the ask. And, of course, the belief that you will never give up no matter what obstacles are put in front of you.

As soon as I found out that I would be taking the auction for the Hot Pink Party, I sent an urgent email to my PR friends begging for a killer hot pink dress that I could wear to the auction. Unfortunately, hot pink wasn't on the color trend spectrum that year so only one friend emailed back to say she had an available dress that was due to arrive back at her office the same day as my auction. The day at work was well underway, which meant that the first time I tried on the dress was in my office on the evening of the auction. I prayed that my intern wouldn't break a finger as she tried to close the incredibly tight hot pink dress sample my friend had sent over from their sample closet. "You've got this," I said as I sucked in and finally felt the zipper close. It was straining, but it closed. I tried to breathe a sigh of relief, but with the dress closed, I could barely breathe. *Short breaths only*, I thought, though I was so relieved that I actually had something to wear that I didn't care. In a way it was a blessing that the dress was so tight; I had something to take my mind off the auction. I was all nerves, having barely slept the night before just thinking about getting onstage next to Elizabeth Hurley before Elton John brought down the house.

That night, as I had done so many times before, I slipped out the back door of Christie's in a pair of sky-high heels, heading to the Waldorf. It was a beautiful April night, and it was so warm I didn't even need a coat. I had given myself ample time to walk from Rockefeller Center to the Waldorf. I didn't feel rushed, which was a positive since I was already taking very shallow breaths because of the dress. As I walked, I reviewed the details for the auction lots on the piece of paper I was holding. I was so busy trying to take shallow breaths while walking and reading my auction notes that I didn't pay attention to anything in front of me, which, if you live in New York, is never a good idea. It is an especially bad idea if you are wearing a pair of high-heel shoes. One second, I was walking down the street, and the next second the entire heel of my shoe had gone through the top of a subway grate. I looked down, praying that it hadn't torn the fabric on the back of my shoe. As I pulled my foot up, I heard a loud pop.

Oh my God, I thought. *This can't be happening. I've just ruined the entire heel of my shoe.* If only that had been the case. It was actually even worse. As I glanced back at the heel of my shoe, I felt sick. The sound wasn't the fabric of the shoe ripping, as I had originally thought. It was the sound of the heel of my shoe snapping. It was 8:15 at night, I was going onstage in exactly forty-five minutes. I had two choices: sit down in the middle of Park Avenue and cry or keep going and figure it out. This was a make-or-break auction for me, and I wasn't going to let this chance slip by. Also, there was no other option. You can't just toss someone else onstage if the auctioneer doesn't show up. But as I looked down at my shoe, I realized that the fabric was holding the heel on the shoe; there was literally nothing else holding it on there. Given the fact that I was due onstage shortly, there was almost no time for me to find another shoe store or construct a shoe out of papier-mâché or drop to my knees and start crying. I did the only thing I could think to do: I ripped off the heel with the fabric, tucked the extra fabric under my foot into the shoe, and walked on my toe across the street into the Waldorf as I desperately tried to figure out what to do.

Dinner was already underway, and the elegant and lovely founder of the auction, Evelyn Lauder, greeted me and ushered me to her table where everyone from Elizabeth Hurley and Monica Seles to Donna Karan and Martha Stewart sat enjoying their dinner. Since the auction was a few minutes late, she let me sit at her place as she greeted all the guests. I felt positively ill. I was missing the heel of a shoe. Fine to pretend that it was there as I walked into a room full of people, not fine to walk onstage in front of a thousand people on my tiptoe. But what do you do in an unwinnable situation? You pivot. And you never give up. I was still sitting there weighing my options when the event planner came over to tell me that the auction would start in roughly thirty minutes. As she leaned over, I smiled and whispered, "This is kind of a random question, but what is your shoe size?"

She looked at me quizzically. "Seven and a half."

"Do you think anyone on your team wears an eight and a half or a nine?"

She looked me like I was crazy. I pulled my shoe out from underneath the tablecloth and pointed at the bottom. "Oh noooo," she said.

"I don't care what color they are, as long as I can get my feet into them."

Two minutes later she was back with a pair of shoes from someone on her team, fifteen minutes later I was onstage raising hundreds of thousands of dollars for breast cancer research. The event was everything I thought it would be and more. I walked offstage feeling like I had reached the peak of my career after I sold a shopping experience with Elizabeth Hurley for fifty thousand dollars and she hugged me onstage, but as I said earlier in this chapter, it was the beginning of a long climb. There have been many other auctions that have come up over the course of my career that seemed like the new zenith, only for me to realize that there was more to come on the other side.

There will be times when obstacles are thrown in your way to stop you in your tracks, to keep you from succeeding, to make the impossible seem exactly that, impossible. But we have the ability to rewrite the story. Even if I got onstage that night with a missing heel, it would have been part of the story. Something was learned. Something was gained. Nothing was lost. And now, whenever there is a wardrobe malfunction, I take it in stride and don't let it stop me.

Never give up applies to every part of our life. If you approach every obstacle with the same "nothing is going to stop me" attitude, you will become the most confident version of yourself. By facing small challenges and applying that attitude when the stakes are low, you are preparing yourself for the greater challenges that will continue over the course of your life. For me, it was learned as a middle school athlete where my enthusiasm was greater than my ability. For you, it will look completely different. The next time you find yourself in a situation where you aren't certain you will succeed, try it anyway, and be okay if it doesn't turn out the way you thought it might. There will always be another opportunity to try again if you never give up.

Claiming your confidence means you never give up, no matter what comes at you. The next time an obstacle seems unsurmountable, know that it isn't. It's only insurmountable if you stop trying or walk away and don't try to pivot in a new direction. Side note: if you ever break your heel at a party and need an extra pair of shoes, just ask around, you never know who might lend you a shoe when you need it the most.

TRISH McEVOY

Founder of Trish McEvoy Beauty

"Never give up" is my philosophy of life. Never give up on your dream. Never give up on your power to make a difference with that dream. You need to make a plan, however, to achieve your dream. Plans need consistency and discipline—and faith in yourself. That's where the power comes from—believing in yourself and believing in your visualization. You also must believe that in the universe, when one door closes, another will open. Because you will face no and all kinds of rejection. I have faced a world of them building my business. I still do. That's because when you ask why, you can learn so much from the no. However tough the road, you can't give up on yourself. Never let others' opinions become your opinion. That's giving your power away. Ask, learn, and evolve—absolutely—but make sure to keep going. And don't be afraid to take risks, even big ones. I always ask "what's the worst that can happen?" I laugh, and then it loses its power to stop me.

3

ASK FOR FORGIVENESS,
NOT FOR PERMISSION

How many times in the past week have you asked someone, "Do you think it is okay if I . . . ?" and then listened so intently someone would think they were doling out the number to a winning lottery number instead of an opinion about how you should live your life? How many times have you wanted to try something new or do something out of your comfort zone only to stop short because you think you should consult someone else?

Indulge me for just one minute.

Pull out a piece of paper.

It's okay if you feel ridiculous, you are claiming your confidence, so you have to get comfortable with the uncomfortable.

I want you to write something down. Write in big, bold, black letters across the piece of paper:

I GIVE MYSELF PERMISSION

Put this piece of paper in a prominent place where you can

reference it anytime. I want to ensure that you remember this phrase because I want you to repeat it every single day when you get out of bed, when you have moments of self-doubt, or when you find yourself pulling out your phone to text someone "Do you think I could/can/should . . . ?" Or, when you find yourself saying the words "Do you think I could . . . ?" The sooner you realize that confidence comes from taking ownership of your own decisions—good or bad—the sooner you will realize that by asking other people for permission to live life, you are letting someone else take control of your life.

When I left my small town of Lake Charles, Louisiana, to go to high school in Watertown, Connecticut, at the age of thirteen, I didn't really grasp the enormity of what leaving home really meant. Whenever I told anyone in my hometown that I was headed to a high school that took two planes, a taxi, and a train to get to, they were certain I had committed a crime or been so naughty that my parents were shipping me off. The real reason was less nefarious: my mother is British and was in boarding school at the age of eight. When my siblings and I were growing up, my mom would regale us with bedtime stories of things that she had done when she was in boarding school—sneaking into the school cafeteria for midnight feasts, shoving snow on a not-so-nice teacher as she walked under the wall at school one day. It all sounded so exciting. I romanticized the idea of leaving home for high school and relentlessly lobbied my parents until they agreed to let me apply. I was accepted, and months later we arrived at the beautiful campus of the Taft School on a crisp fall September day. It was a complete departure from the oppressive heat and humidity of early fall in Louisiana. The leaves on the trees of the campus were edged with yellows and reds that were so different from the year-round green that I left at home, a sure sign that summer was over and it was time for school to begin again.

As my parents helped move me into the room that would be my home for the next year, the enormity of the fact I was about to be left by myself began to sink in. Trying to hold back tears as we unpacked my clothes and organized my belongings in my tiny room, I realized that I might have bitten off more than I could chew.

I remember two things very vividly in those first few weeks at school: First, the immediate void that came from not having the physical presence of my parents as part of my everyday life. That void was quickly filled by the nonstop schedule that consumed every minute of the day. Classes took place Monday through Saturday, with sports or extracurricular activities occupying every afternoon. After classes we ran to sports, after sports we ran down to our dorms for a quick shower, followed by a school-wide meeting every night called vespers, then off to a seated dinner. We moved so quickly and efficiently from space to space that the only time I had to really think about missing my parents was at night after lights went out. I have never been a good sleeper, so at night I would read books for hours trying to ward off the homesickness until I fell asleep.

The second thing I remember was the void of decisions no longer made by my parents; the space they had previously occupied with their opinions and advice. Before I left home, my first stop for a general question about history or anything related to the physical world was my dad. If he didn't know, he would pick up an encyclopedia (you might have to google that word if you were born after

2000) and find the answer. And if he couldn't find it, he would likely just make it up. Anything about life in general was a question for my mom; from the practical to the personal, she seemed to always know the answer. In today's world, if I have a question, I simply text them or give them a quick call. It's so easy to get their life advice. But when I was in high school there were no cell phones; there was a much more circuitous route to get answers. That route came in the form of a single pay phone one flight of stairs up from my room. There were sixteen girls in the dorm and exactly one phone we used to call home, a boyfriend, or anyone else with whom we wanted to speak. In my first year, by the time I waited in line to call home, I would often forget what I meant to ask my parents. Calls home were more of a catch-up session where I could tell my parents the gossip at school and find out what was going on at home. In short, if I needed an answer to a burning question at an odd hour of the day, I had to come up with that answer or find someone else who might know the answer. As a result, at the age of thirteen I learned an invaluable lesson: the importance of independent thinking and having confidence in those decisions.

What I learned at an early age is how to shut out the white noise of other people's thoughts and opinions in favor of your own. You won't always be right by any stretch of the imagination. There have been many times when I listened to my own opinions and paid for it dearly. Even two decades into my career I've made decisions that I wish I'd handled differently. I'm not sure there is enough room in this book to list every single one of the decisions that I made that did not work out as I planned. But I also learned that if I gave myself permission to make those decisions, I could only blame myself if things did not turn out the way I wanted them to turn out. I claimed ownership of my life no matter how things turned out, which, I realized, is what it takes to live life on your terms.

As with a lot of people who move to New York City in their early twenties, I always knew I would live in New York. And like many other people who move to New York to live out their dreams, I moved to the city on a prayer and a shoestring paycheck. I lived in "penthouse apartments" from the minute I moved to New York City because I always lived on the top floor. "Penthouse apartment" was my positive mindset at work, as my apartments were typically at the top of five flights of stairs. My first few years of living in New York were complete with all the pitfalls of most early twenty-year-olds trying to find their footing in the NYC housing market. I leased from one person, and she decided to move back early—a rooming situation fell through the day before I was supposed to move in. One roommate turned out to be less than ideal, so I lived with a friend's parents for a month until finally, a stroke of luck.

One night after work I hopped the train to meet up with my best friend who was living in Stamford, Connecticut, a city about an hour by train outside of New York. We hadn't seen each other in months and decided to meet halfway between NYC and Stamford for dinner. Over too many glasses of cheap wine to count, she expressed how she was ready to leave her job and move to San Francisco. Why San Francisco? I asked. Why don't you just move to New York? Fair warning: don't ever tell me you want to move to New York unless you are ready for the full-court press. Within a month she had quit her job and found a new job working at a top financial company in the city and we were combing the *New York Times* real estate section looking at every penthouse apartment in Manhattan. After viewing roughly twenty-five apartments and walking approximately a thousand flights of stairs, we signed a lease on a fifth-floor walk-up. Since the majority of our money was going toward rent, we didn't have money for gym memberships, so we figured it would be a good way to get our dose of daily exercise and joked it would only serve to firm and tone on a daily basis.

The day after we signed the lease, we ran to the apartment, measuring tape in hand, to figure out where we would fit our belongings. Since my friend had a job at a bank and was making three times more than me, she took the bigger bedroom in exchange for paying more rent. We measured her room first and then pulled out the tape measure for my room. As I yelled out the measurements to my room, she started howling with laughter. I walked out of the room to look at her and she said, "Do you realize your room is exactly the same size as your mattress?" My bedroom fit exactly one thing, my mattress. To get dressed in the morning I would simply roll over, slide open the closet door, remove my clothes, and leave my room. It was, without a doubt, one of the best years of my life.

The side benefit of living with someone so financially savvy was that I received free advice simply by mentioning all the financial mistakes I was making on a daily basis. Unlike me, she had a good grasp of finance and would parcel out advice when I made comments like, "You don't really need to pay off the minimum on your credit card." Her jaw dropped. "YES, LYDIA! You absolutely do need to pay off your minimum on your credit card otherwise you will ruin your credit for seven years. She was right; trust me on this one. Or the first time I received a three-hundred-dollar bonus at work and spent the entire amount on a pair of shoes before I even received the direct deposit into my account. I wasn't aware that taxes would take away almost half of that money. She took the time to patiently explain everything she could think of that might set me up for success in life and answered questions that I didn't even know to ask.

While she had everything in complete control in her own life, there was one thing I noticed immediately; she still felt the need to ask for permission whenever making decisions. There was no doubt that my friend was eminently responsible, definitely more so than me. She had saved enough money to purchase the apartment in Stamford while she was living there, so she was now a landlord in addition to acting as my unofficial financial advisor and roommate. But as we sat on our living room floor eating takeout one night, it occurred to me that even though she was in charge of her life, she didn't realize she was really in charge of her life.

The discussion that night was about her new role as a landlord. Her new tenants were moving into her now rented apartment, and she needed to get the apartment repainted. My first suggestion was that we pick up some paint and go out and paint it ourselves. I had painted all of my dorm rooms in college, not all successfully, I might add, so her concerns about me moonlighting as her painter were spot-on. She called her father to discuss options as I listened from the mattress, aka my bedroom. I could hear her talking about the expense of the painter he was suggesting versus the super in the building who could do it for half the price. While it was clear she felt the super could do a good job, by the end of the conversation he told her that she needed to use the painter he suggested. Never one to keep my opinions to myself, I waited until she hung up the phone and asked her point-blank, "Who is paying for this?"

To which she replied, "I am."

"Well then, why are you calling your dad to figure this out? You are twenty-four and bought an apartment. He can give you advice, but you don't need his permission anymore. You have a job, you make your own money, if you want to hire a cheaper painter, hire a cheaper painter."

She looked me dead in the eye. "I honestly never thought about it that way."

I still think about that conversation all the time. Why do women in particular feel like we constantly need to ask if we can do anything? Why do we always feel like we need to seek the validation of others to make decisions in our lives? Why do we stop short of going after things because we worry about the opinions of others?

As women we are often raised to believe that we need validation from other people to move forward with our goals or to live life on our own terms. In fact, the only person from whom you need validation is yourself. If you are confident in who you are and what you want from your life, you can ask other people their opinion, but ultimately their opinion should be weighted far less than yours. The next time you ask someone a question about something in your life, stop yourself and make it a statement. Deep down you likely have the answer, but by getting an outside opinion you are simply showing everyone you aren't capable of making a decision. Trust that when you bring your whole self to each decision, you can make those decisions better than anyone else. Also remember that you are creating your life story each and every day, so be proud of that story and realize that if you give yourself permission to create your life story, you have ownership of every moment of your life.

Wherever you are in your journey, whether just embarking on your career, navigating life as a parent, or beginning your life as an adult, remember that living in truth will allow you to live a life where you don't need to ask for permission. There were so many times in my early twenties, before I felt confident, when I didn't feel comfortable owning the fact that I was at the beginning of my journey. I always felt like I needed to excuse the fact that I was just starting out, that I needed to apologize for the hustle. I was living in a fifth-floor walk-up with my best friend while working at the world's top auction house where a single painting sold for millions of dollars. I was, quite frankly, embarrassed by the climb without realizing that the climb is where you learn every skill you will apply over the course of your life. What I didn't know then that I know now is that there is no top of the mountain without the climb, without the beginning of the story. In time you will realize that the first chapters of your story *make* you into who you are today. When you listen to any of the greats tell their story, they never tell the story about being at the top of the mountain, they tell the story of how they got there. When you hear Oprah talk about the first years of her career as a talk show host, she is candid about the struggle, about what she learned from it. She talks about the mistakes she made in those early years in her career, the questions that she asked that came across in a way that she didn't intend or the conversations she had that she wished had gone another way. But she learned and she grew every time she made a mistake, instead of letting those moments stop her from moving forward. The beginning is the training ground where you learn what you are worth and prove your ability to go after your dreams. It's also where you become comfortable enough in your own skin that you stop asking permission from other people about what you should do with your life.

Although I knew this to be true, in my first decade at Christie's I felt like the confidence that I had gained in myself, in independent thought, was challenged at every turn. Offices have structures, ladders, and cultures that can challenge even the strongest independent thinkers. Since I had started so early in my career, I found myself bending to the culture time and time again to stay in line and do what was expected. It wasn't until a decade into my career that I heard the phrase that encapsulated an entire shift in my life. In 2011, before sustainability became the buzzword of the decade, one of my colleagues noticed a trend in the nonprofit interests of our clients. While our clients had traditionally supported charitable endeavors like cancer research or arts education in schools, we noticed that they were becoming increasingly focused on climate change. To support our clients, a small team came together to conceptualize an auction benefitting four nonprofits whose mission it was to improve issues around climate change. Held on Earth Day, we called it "Christie's Green Auction: A Bid to Save the Earth." Why be subtle, right?

Our team was led by our global head of communications, a take-charge no-nonsense man with a heart of gold who looks strikingly similar to Bruce Willis. He seemed to be completely unafraid of anything, anyone, or asking for anything. As a woman who was in her early thirties, gripped with imposter syndrome and worried about another person's perception of me, I was completely amazed. I had only recently transitioned from my role as head of events to start my new department, strategic partnerships. In my new role I often felt uncomfortable with my new level of seniority and would still get nervous raising my hand in a room full of senior executives. It was clear from our first meetings that the new global head of communications did not share in this concern. Not only did he never take no for an answer, but in hindsight, I think he almost felt galvanized by a negative response.

One day, the team was sitting around the large round table in our boardroom and we started brainstorming names for potential hosts for the Green Auction, the event of the season. We all gave a few suggestions for people we might be able to ask, while he rattled off increasingly impressive names. All of a sudden he was quiet. Then he blurted out, "I'm going to call the White House and see if Michelle Obama can host." I remember laughing along with the rest of the committee. I might have a touch of delusional optimism, but even I thought the First Lady was completely out of reach. Yet a week later when we reconvened for our next meeting, he proudly announced that he had somehow secured the name of Michelle Obama's chief of staff with whom he was corresponding about her attendance at the event. We weren't laughing anymore.

After the meeting I hung back and asked him how he was able to obtain the email address for someone who knew the First Lady. He told me he had emailed every person that he had ever met, and even people he didn't know, asking if they knew of anyone who might be able to make an introduction. One person had offered an email to someone else who offered an email, and he followed the thread until he found his person. As we walked back to his office I said, "I am incredibly impressed that you were able to get to Michelle Obama." He smiled right at me and said, "Ask for forgiveness, not for permission, Lydia." It hit me like a lightning bolt. I don't know if I had heard the phrase before, but when I heard it that day, I realized that as long as I live I would never forget it.

Why not ask the question? Why not be confident enough in yourself to believe that no one in the world is beyond your reach, even if that is not the case? When we ultimately received the email saying that she would not be able to make the event, I remember what he said to our team. "That's okay. Better to have her say no than not to have asked." The most remarkable part was that he didn't live his life fearing he would get in trouble for asking someone a question.

Ask for forgiveness, not for permission. His words galvanized me. I poured through my contact lists emboldened by this phrase. If I stopped believing I needed permission to ask, what more could I accomplish? How would I stop holding myself back? What would hold any of us back if we believed we can do whatever we want, ask whatever we want, live however we want? In a word: nothing.

Within the day I was emailing and calling people I had met at events or charity auctions that I would never have reached out to before having that conversation. The first year of our benefit was an unmitigated success. We raised a million dollars to benefit four nonprofits focused on saving the planet. Building on the success of the first year, we decided to hold a second event the following year, and using the same philosophy I was able to secure *Vogue* as a partner for the event. It was a magical night; Anna Wintour sat in the front row with Graydon Carter, the high-powered editor of *Vanity Fair* magazine, while Nicki Minaj performed at the event. I took the auction stage as the auctioneer alongside my junior charity auctioneer trainee Seth Myers, and together we raised over one million dollars at the event. The event was incredible, and by simply giving myself permission to make those asks, I had been part of the team that made it incredible. It was another important tool in my ever-growing toolbox, and one you should start using the minute you put down this book. If you aren't asking anyone for permission, you have nothing holding you back.

Also remember that when you start asking for anything and everything you *will* hear the word no. You need to learn to not only expect this, but embrace that it is part of being fearless with your ask. I have learned that the first no will always sting, but the rest will sting less. I know this from experience. Rest assured that when you hear the word no, you are in good company. Mine.

When I was writing *The Most Powerful Woman in the Room Is You*, my editor suggested that we try to bring in points of view from other women about the messages in the book by including case studies. To do this, I compiled a wish list of sixty women from all walks of life whom I had admired over the years because of their business acumen, their work in the nonprofit sector, or simply their perspective. Think a combined list of the most influential women in the world and the Forbes 100 list. I felt confident in the ask. I was writing a book called *The Most Powerful Woman in the Room Is You*. Who wouldn't want to be included, right?

I remember sitting in front of my computer in my apartment with the complete list of power women in front of me alongside the relevant email addresses or IG handles I had compiled from Instagram. I started at the top of the list. Go big or go home, right? The first email was going to a famous news anchor. We had met briefly at a "Ladies Who Don't Lunch" lunch years before (an annual Christmastime event held in the 21 Club's private wine cellar), but given the fact that she was an international celebrity I doubted she would remember me. I stared at the screen feeling the rush of adrenaline I always feel when I am nervous. I got up, walked around the apartment, and came back to sit down in front of the computer. I felt like I needed to slam down my gavel before I sent the first email. I also remember feeling as though I should ask someone before I sent the email, before thinking how silly it was that I should need that kind of validation.

Ask for forgiveness, not for permission.

There it was . . . that internal push-pull that always seems to happen when venturing out of my comfort zone.

I am sending an email to someone I don't know, asking for a quote.

She is a person; I am a person.

You've got this, I thought.

Deep breath in, deep breath out, I closed my eyes and hit send. After the familiar *whoosh* indicated the email was leaving my inbox, I felt emboldened. I started sending the emails to the other people on the list in rapid-fire succession. I worked quickly until I heard the *ding* of an email in my inbox. I almost gasped when I saw the name of the TV personality in my inbox. I smiled, confident that the fact that she had responded so quickly meant that the message would be positive. After all, it had only taken her ten minutes to respond.

The email was kind, but short. Unfortunately, she was unable to promote my book because of a clause in her contract. I felt like I had been punched in the stomach. I could feel the spiral of negativity and a little panic as well. What if no one wanted to be in the book? What if I couldn't get anyone to say yes to participating in a case study? Not the greatest feeling in the world.

That was it. She said no. It didn't feel great, but I was still alive and breathing after I read the email. After the first sting of rejection, the rest barely registered. It was as if the first no packed the punch and everything after that felt less impactful.

I left my computer and went for a run. By the time I came back I had a number of email responses. The first one was from Barbara Corcoran's assistant. She would be delighted to do it and would send her quote shortly. I let out a shriek and ran to tell my husband. After the first email I received some fantastic emails saying yes as well, along with a whole lot of NO responses. Out of my initial list of sixty asks, fifteen women said yes, forty-five said no. Should I repeat that for you again in case you are feeling discouraged about going

after something you want? Three-quarters of the people I asked said no. I could easily have focused on that, but instead I chose to focus on the positive: one-quarter said yes! And that is a good start.

I realized that to get the case studies in on deadline, I would need to expand my reach. I thought back to the Green Auction and my colleague reaching out to Michelle Obama. I decided to do the same. I went through my contacts and sent an email to my friends asking two questions: (1) Who was the most powerful woman they had ever met or knew, and (2) Would they feel comfortable connecting me to that person or passing along their email address? If you read *The Most Powerful Woman in the Room Is You*, you will notice there are thirty-three case studies. Half were my contacts, and half were the contacts of my contacts. All of them were in the book because I asked. Not for permission. I gave myself permission to make those asks.

There was one other thing I noticed when I was sending out the asks for case studies to the original group of sixty women. When I reached out to ask if they would provide a case study, a few women immediately asked for a list of other women who were providing case studies, as if they needed to be sure that they would be in the right company as case study participants in the book. I thought back on this after the fact because there were three women who never asked that question. Three women whose names are household names and had nothing to gain by being in my book: Martha Stewart, Deborah Roberts, and Barbara Corcoran. It occurred to me that is the epitome of confidence. When you are so comfortable in your skin that you don't ask who else is involved in a project or some-

thing where you are asked to lend your name. You are there and that is enough. Those women aren't looking from side to side trying to figure out what other people are doing, they just do what they want to do. They don't ask for permission, they live life on their terms no matter what other people may think or say about their decisions, and they own it. It taught me a lesson about what it truly means to be confident in yourself.

After my book was published, other authors asked me to include pieces in their book. If I wanted to participate, I simply said yes, no questions asked. I also said no to a few asks because another part of asking for permission is understanding that you are not required to do anything you don't want to do. You can give yourself permission to do the things you want to do just as you can choose to do the opposite. The next time someone asks you to do something, step up and own your space without asking who else is involved. You are enough without anyone else. Let that be your permission slip in life.

A few months ago, I met a young woman at a book signing. Book signings are my favorite part about writing a book; I get to meet so many people and learn so much from each question or comment. I drive the bookstore owners crazy because I want to have long conversations with each and every person in line. During this book signing, I noticed a young woman who had waited patiently at the very end of the book signing line. It was clear from her behavior that she had questions and didn't want to be rushed.

As I handed her the first book she said, "I noticed from your IG account that you live in Tribeca, I live in Tribeca too." Making small talk, I asked what most New Yorkers ask if you mention that

you live in their neighborhood, so you can compare notes on your favorite coffee shop or deli. "Where do you live?" I said. She immediately turned bright red and became flustered. "Well, I live in this building that isn't that great." Her response triggered something in me that I can't explain—maybe because I spent so many of my early years at work trying to gloss over the fact that *I* lived in a walk-up when I was working at a place where such immense wealth was part of my every day. Or simply nodding when people said, "Lydia comes from New Orleans," instead of correcting them as I do now when I immediately say, "No—I grew up in Lake Charles, not New Orleans," because somehow coming from New Orleans made me feel like I was more deserving of a seat at the table.

I felt compelled to say to her what I wish I could have said to myself so many times over the years: "Don't ever apologize for the hustle. You live in the greatest city in the world. Be so proud of where you live because you are doing it. We all started in a fifth-floor walk-up—that's what makes it so much sweeter when you finally get the apartment you always dreamed of because you made it happen. The hustle is the best part."

She teared up and grabbed my arm. "Thank you so much for saying that," she said. "I can't tell you how much it means to hear that." I doubt she was expecting such an earful, but I hope you also feel free when you read those words. You are who you are and that is enough. To live in your truth means you aren't worried about what others think of your journey. Be proud of where you are and what you are doing. If you aren't, give yourself permission to change it.

In this era of influencers and social media, and an endless

stream of sources which imply that we can all be perfect in every facet of our life every hour of every day, remember that you will never feel as confident as you do when you are living life in your truth. If you are living your life in truth, you will never have to fear that someone can out you for being a fraud. You will never have to avoid someone or cut short a conversation because something you said doesn't hold up. As a close friend of mine often says in response to a huge reveal, "Well, the cards are on the table, and they're all faceup." If you make sure that your cards are always faceup in life, you will feel confident in who you are.

Life is not linear; success is not guaranteed. It will come to some earlier than others. Don't make excuses, don't try to gloss over your past to make people think you are something you are not. You cannot live a confident life if you are constantly waiting for someone to find out what you are saying about yourself isn't true. Once you realize this and own your confidence you will quickly realize you don't need permission to make your own choices and live life the way you want to live it.

The next time you find yourself asking, "Should I do this? Say this?"—claim your confidence.

Pull out the sheet of paper that says "I GIVE MYSELF PERMISSION" and shout it from the rooftop.

And on the days when you aren't feeling like you want to give yourself permission, feel free to put an asterisk next to your permission slip and add at the bottom:

*Lydia gives me permission, too.

Because I will. Always.

RACHELLE HRUSKA

Founder of Lingua Franca

After a suggestion from a therapist that I "find something I can do with my hands" to combat my postpartum depression, I picked up an old sweater and hand stitched "booyah" across it.

Little did I know the Instagram photo that followed would be the start of a new company and life-fulfilling journey.

A couple months after my post, I had several major department stores—including Net-a-Porter, my north star—reach out via DM to carry the line. The only problem? I didn't have a "line" . . . per say. I was stitching on old vintage cashmeres, adding a "lingua franca" hang tag to them, posting them to IG, and then selling them to chic clientele at my husband's restaurant, The Crow's Nest, in Montauk. At one point I had to stop embroidering on vintage Ralph Lauren cashmere sweaters after receiving a robust cease-and-desist letter hand delivered to my home (whoops!).

Still, I ended up taking a call with the head buyer for Net-a-Porter on the Fourth of July in 2016. It was at 4:00 a.m. (she in London, me in Malibu), and I'll never forget it.

When she explained that she wanted to be the first to carry our brand online, it meant that we would have to send her desired order of 1,500 sweaters (all hand embroidered).

Instead of telling her the truth, that we didn't really have a

brand—there was no supplier, no embroiderers (save for myself and a woman, Kate, who I had found on Craigslist earlier that summer), and no real "plan"—I told her "YES!" We could totally make this work.

In the end, we did make it work. Well, sort of. I hustled around Los Angeles finding a cashmere supplier, while Kate worked away in NYC finding embroiderers. That summer was a wild blur. We completed closer to half of her desired order, and cut off some phrases, but we did it, and the sweaters sold out in less than a week. This was the official start of our company, which since that point has almost thirty employees, four store locations, and has donated over one million dollars to charities.

Years after my cease-and-desist letter, I'll never forget walking with Kate (now our COO) into the flagship Ralph Lauren building to meet with the global head of design and team to discuss a potential collaboration together. "You know, I got my start embroidering on vintage RL cashmeres . . . until you guys put an end to that!"

4

SLAM YOUR
IMPOSTER SYNDROME

One of my favorite lines in a song comes from—wait for it—Katy Perry's "Roar": "I stood for nothing, so I fell for everything," which is a cue for my youngest daughter to sprint to her costume pile, and the rest of my family to start dancing like crazy around our house. Anytime I am in a situation where I feel like keeping my hand down instead of raising it or swallowing a comment because I felt like my voice wasn't the most important one in the room, I remember that line. If you don't stand up for yourself, you are allowing someone else to choose your path. It's only when you find your voice and stand your ground that you realize you always had the ability to do it, you just had to stand up for yourself. As often happens in my life, I learned this lesson the hard way, as a charity auctioneer.

Tell me if this sounds familiar. You walk into a meeting filled with people of all ages and genders. This scenario doesn't have to be in an office, it could be a classroom, a town hall, or even a Zoom meeting. Once the meeting begins, you immediately start thinking, *What am I doing here? Everyone here knows so much more than I do.* As the meeting progresses, any comments or thoughts that you planned to share remain exactly that, thoughts, because if you open your mouth, you worry that everyone will remember you aren't supposed to be at the table in the first place. What starts as a feeling that stops us from putting our hand up in a meeting only gets worse as we get further into our lives. This feeling might stop us from putting our hand up for a promotion, a raise, or for anything at all. Over time it evolves from a feeling to a deep-seated belief that we aren't meant to be in the room, sitting in the boardroom or anywhere near the building, for that matter. Talk to any woman who has been in the working world or in a leadership position in the past two decades and I guarantee she can tell you all about imposter syndrome. She might not know it by name, but I assure you most women reading this page are probably nodding along. Imposter syndrome is a feeling that stops many of us, notably women, in our tracks. It keeps many of us from getting into the room where we would have the chance to fail.

In the working world it is even more obvious. As you ascend the corporate ladder, no matter how deserving you are of a new title, a raise, a new position, you may never truly believe you deserve any of it. When you look around a room of your peers, even if you know you deserve to be there, there is always a little voice inside telling you that you are lucky to be in that room. I can't tell you where I first heard the phrase, but from the minute I heard it, I knew exactly what it meant: *I am an imposter in this world of successful people. I don't deserve any of this, and at some point, this whole house of cards, despite the fact that it is built on my accomplishments, will come falling down. It's only a matter of time.*

Do you, perhaps, feel seen?

Fear not, my friend, I'm here to tell you, you aren't alone. Imposter syndrome is omnipresent.

When I have speaking engagements, I always enjoy the Q & A's. It is the opportunity for people to engage on a more personal level, and it takes away the formality of a speech and allows you to get a little more personal. I keep a notebook filled with questions that people ask so that I can think about the questions after the speech. When I look through that notebook there are two questions that are asked at least half of the time: "Do you suffer from imposter syndrome?" followed immediately by "How do you get rid of it?"

In the words of Gen-Zers everywhere, there is so much to unpack here. So, let's unpack the whole suitcase. The first answer is, OF COURSE. Of course I suffer from imposter syndrome. I am not only a woman, but a woman who grew up in an industry that was filled with women in support roles with men holding all the senior and C-suite titles. I never wanted to have imposter syndrome; in fact, until I heard the phrase, I didn't know that anyone else felt the same way. I didn't know that other women felt like they weren't taken seriously, that their opinions mattered less, or that people were always dismissing them whenever they were in meetings. I didn't realize that other women who were at the top of their game always felt like they shouldn't be there. But how could we not?

The narrative that I was not as capable as my male peers was messaged to me throughout my life and my career. The stories from the earliest days of my working life include so many moments that make me cringe two decades into my career: how many times I was told I was lucky to have my job; how asking for more money was considered tacky; how even as a senior leader in the company, if I was the only woman in the room, I would always be asked to minute the meeting. When I recount this to my guy friends they laugh in disbelief. I assure you that not one of them was ever told that they were lucky go to work, nor were they asked to do the work of an assistant in front of a crowded room of their peers. They were expected to go to work to provide for their family. Going to work was something they were born to do. Even though I lived off my salary, I always felt that people believed my career was simply a brief stop on my way to getting married and "settling down." There were so many other subliminal messages that helped reinforce this belief. I went to an office where, despite the fact that women were the majority, we were never in the top roles. I didn't need to feel that by doing my best the chance for a senior role was limited at best; I could see it right in front of me. That doesn't even factor in the constant jokes about women with children never working as hard or as well as others. Spoiler alert: we can, and we can do it well, thanks for asking!

As a result, I spent many years on the sidelines watching guys on a fast track to success, while I was still thanking everyone for my meager paycheck and the opportunity to work for my company. I was led to believe that even at my best I was still less than or not enough, and that I should always defer to the loudest person in the room, despite the fact that many times the loudest person was wrong. All of this meant that, with thousands of auctions under my belt, I would still find myself backstage with celebrities or luminaries thinking, *What on earth am I doing here?* instead of *Yes, this makes sense. I've done the work, put in the hours, run the charity auction team at the world's leading auction house, so of course I should be here.* It wasn't until I started to stand up for what I believed in, started to force myself to speak up in meetings no matter how uncomfortable I felt, and *stopped* looking for outside affirmation that my imposter syndrome began to dissipate. I no longer look around to figure out what I am doing in the room or if I should be there. I am in the room because I deserve it. I believe it, and THAT is what matters.

The answer to the second question is more complicated. How did you get rid of it? I don't know that we can ever fully get rid of it, but being aware of it and speaking openly helps us learn to control it and normalize the feeling for others around us. I also realized that the place where imposter syndrome is the loudest is in my head. I wish that I could say that I no longer had any imposter syndrome, ever. That I can walk into any room or any place and never feel that slight uptick in my nerves. That would not be true. But the difference now is that I don't let that voice paralyze me anymore. I don't let it stop me from speaking up or making my voice heard. I have a number of tips for conquering imposter syndrome, but the biggest one is that you have to realize no one else can make it go away. The only person who can get rid of it is you. It takes work, almost daily, as a reminder that to be confident you not only need to believe in yourself, but you can't look outside yourself to seek that affirmation from anyone else. Truth be told, in the meetings, when you are looking around the room thinking, *I don't belong here*, everyone else is sitting around the table thinking, *What am I having for lunch?*

To rid yourself of imposter syndrome, remember one key fact: People are rarely thinking about you at all. Conversations about who you are and what you are doing are usually not the topic of someone else's day. If they are, consider it gossip and ignore it. If you want to completely rid yourself of imposter syndrome, you need to claim your space and create the narrative about the life you are living. If you are constantly looking to other people to create the narrative of your life, of course you have imposter syndrome. You aren't living the life you want to live. Fill the chapters of your life's book with words and actions that define who you want to be and message that to other people. By telling other people who you are and what you stand for, you are telling other people what you think about yourself. Once you claim ownership over your life and your life story, you will stop worrying about being an imposter. Confidence comes when you realize that it doesn't matter what anyone else thinks about you. It's what you think about yourself that matters. It's not until you truly believe in YOU that you will be able to break free of that syndrome and step into your most confident self.

You might be thinking this is easier said than done. How do you address it? How do you tackle the fear that you don't belong? How do you gain confidence in yourself to believe that not only do you belong in the room, but that you can be in control and command of the room?

I like to call it "the Slam," your foolproof "I've got this," "this is my life and I'm going to rock it" line of defense against imposter syndrome. Just like I slam my gavel down when I walk onstage to show everyone I mean business, the Slam will make sure that you slam the door on imposter syndrome anytime it tries to sneak back into your thoughts and convince you that you are anything less than a rock star. You know it and I know it too.

So, let's get started getting your Slam ready so everyone, including you, knows that you mean business.

1. **S**—STOP counting yourself out.
2. **L**—LISTEN to what someone is saying, not what you think they are saying.
3. **A**—ACCEPT that no one will give you a gold star.
4. **M**—MAKE your point and stand your ground.

STOP COUNTING YOURSELF OUT

The first letter in the Slam Method is S for STOP. Stop before you start. Don't count yourself out of the game before the game has even started. The next time someone offers you a position, an honor, or gives you a compliment, just STOP. Stop talking, stop overexplaining and trying to explain away the reason you have been given something. From now on, strip away that layer of imposter syndrome by doing the opposite of what you think you should do. Say thank you and STOP talking.

If you want the Slam to work for you, one of the first things you need to imagine is a big, red stop sign that you pull out anytime you find yourself bashfully passing on any opportunity that comes your way. Your answer in life should always be "YES, thank you very much." I can't tell you how many times a high-achieving friend has been put forward for something only to take herself out of the game by immediately listing all the reasons she shouldn't have been considered in the first place, or putting herself down as if to make sure that everyone knows she is likely not worthy of the opportunity. Guess what? If you do this, everyone will think it was a mistake because you just told them that it was a mistake.

My mom was recently asked to join the executive committee for a board she has been working on for many years. "I don't know why they would want me. I don't bring anything to the committee."

What my mom doesn't see in herself, which everyone around her sees as clear as day, is that she has the ability to make everything she touches look beautiful. If you were to ask me to pick flowers out of a garden and put them in a vase, when you return you will get exactly what you asked for—flowers in a vase. If you were lucky enough to give my mom a bundle of flowers and ask her to put them in a vase, you would think the top florist in New York had popped by to arrange flowers while you were gone. When she makes a statement about not knowing why anyone would ask her to join a committee, the only thing I can think is—they would be crazy not to. Anyone would love for her to be on a committee. She should be the CEO of a Fortune 500 company with her people skills. People are drawn to her, so it is no wonder people want her on a committee— she has an incredible eye and a wonderful, positive can-do attitude. They would be lucky to have her there.

I watch women put themselves down like this, count themselves out, dissuade people from promoting them because they don't check every box on the job description. STOP counting yourself out. Get in the game and promote yourself. No one can do it as well as you.

LISTEN TO *WHAT* SOMEONE IS SAYING, NOT WHAT YOU *THINK* THEY ARE SAYING

Tell me if this scenario sounds familiar. You are having a conversation with someone in your life: a friend, someone senior in your office, or someone whose opinion you care deeply about for professional or personal reasons. They mention they are so glad that they get to see you now that your children are getting older and you can be in the office more. As they leave the room you stop cold, your face flush, ice water filling your veins. Your mind takes over and starts creating a storyline based on that comment. Almost like a "choose your own adventure" story gone wrong.

Now let's remember that the person said, "It's great to see you in the office more now that your children are getting older," and you think, *Oh my God. They think that I have been out of the game for years and only now am I getting back into the game. Everyone here thinks that I don't do a good job, that I am just coasting, that I have plateaued. I need to show them. I need to show them I am still good at this job and that I do care. I'll start working on the weekends, do extra work* . . . and on and on you go down a spiral of self-doubt and insecurity about everything that you have ever felt about your job performance or your life performance.

STOP and LISTEN.

What did this person say? "It's great to see you in the office more now that your children are getting older."

Period.

Your answer? "Thanks!"

End scene.

Believe in yourself enough to believe that other people are thinking the best of you, not the worst. And if you want to know what I would do to really Slam that imposter syndrome, I would write my own story.

Let's go back and rewrite that scene, shall we?

What did that person say? "It's great to see you in the office more now that your children are getting older."

Here is what I want you to hear: "You are such a valuable member of this team, it's really great to have your positive energy in this office. Also, you must be an incredible multitasker to be raising kids at home and crushing it at work, too. What a role model for the people around you. We are lucky to have you."

End scene. Cue applause.

ACCEPT THAT NO ONE WILL GIVE YOU A GOLD STAR

When I became an auctioneer at the age of twenty-four, I was not only young, I was a young woman; no one was more aware of that than me. It didn't help that every time I arrived to take an auction, people would look past me in hopes that a more seasoned, male auctioneer would magically appear. Since I was acutely aware that I was not what people were expecting as an auctioneer, which I compensated for by thanking people for letting me take their auction, it is no wonder that I wore my imposter syndrome like a glittering robe for everyone to see. Starting with my very first auction all the way through to my thousandth auction, I was always so *grateful* that someone asked me to take their auction. It never once occurred to me that perhaps an organization might be grateful that I was donating my evenings and weekends, late into the night, to raise money for their cause. While a few of my friends who were male auctioneers would show up with minimal preparation and joke about how many glasses of wine they had consumed before they got onstage, I never, ever touched a glass of anything alcoholic at the event. My biggest fear was if an auction didn't go well, they would blame it on the young, drunk female auctioneer who had no business being there. When I was inevitably seated at the table next to the bathroom, or one of the many times when they forgot to put a seat out for me at the dinner at all, leaving me to sit backstage waiting two hours for an auction to take place, I felt like I deserved it. Who was I, after all? A young woman doing a job meant for an older, more experienced man.

It's not surprising that I wasn't getting respect. I wasn't presenting myself as someone who deserved it. I never offered a point of view or an opinion on any matter related to the auction other than agreeing with what everyone else said. In my mind, being agreeable meant you'd be well liked, and if you were well liked, then things would work out for you. It turns out that strategy didn't really work, because in my beginning years as an auctioneer I was more forgettable than memorable onstage. More often than not when I walked offstage after an auction, I would never even receive a thank-you from the people organizing the event. That lack of acknowledgment only served to feed into my belief that *I* should be thankful that anyone asked me to take their auction.

Over the years, though, as I became more confident in my abilities, I realized that wanting to be liked and always being agreeable was feeding into my imposter syndrome. Similar to the affirmation that I craved as a student who was always first to raise my hand in class, I was living my adult life seeking a gold star that doesn't exist. Once I realized this, I also realized that another trick to rid yourself of imposter syndrome is to accept that there are no gold stars in life. I watch as so many people continue to chase a nonexistent stamp of approval that they will never achieve.

Read this carefully every time you find yourself looking for affirmation: chasing a gold star is a zero-sum game. No one pins a gold star on you for living the life you want as you get older, nor do they withhold it because you are doing what you want to do. There is no A+ written across your monthly calendar at work for a job well done. There is no gold star for being mom of the year because you do the laundry every single day. You aren't competing against anyone but yourself. Stop trying to please other people by doing something in pursuit of a gold star. The only gold star you should seek in your life is the one you give yourself. You know when you have performed your best and given it your all, just as you know when you have had an off day and something didn't go as well as you hoped. Seek your own approval for a job well done. Be confident knowing that giving it your all is what gets you a seat at the table and be comfortable knowing that you deserve to be there with or without the approval of those around you.

Some nights as I get offstage after a long auction where people talk throughout, people like to make comments as I weave back through the crowded room to find my table. Inevitably there is someone who puts their hand on my arm and says, "You did a good job; that was a tough crowd." In my twenties I would have analyzed that comment for hours, mulling it over and over in my head, doubting my ability. It would have given me a knot in my stomach that lasted until the next time I got onstage later that week. Somehow, if the next performance was better, it could help mentally undo the one before and I could try to forget the comment that had kept me up at night. I'm sure you've been there before too. Let me offer this piece of advice. Forget about it and move on. Having learned to bring confidence to a situation instead of imposter syndrome, I don't let it phase me. As long as I walked onto that stage with confidence in my abilities and did my best, I believe that no one could have done it better. Now I simply put my hand on top of theirs and say, "I'm a charity auctioneer; the only crowd I know is a tough crowd." Find your own version of that sentence and let that be your gold star.

MAKE YOUR POINT AND STAND YOUR GROUND

If you really want to rid yourself of imposter syndrome for good, you have to learn to stand your ground. There are going to be so many times when you encounter differing opinions or viewpoints. You will not always be right, but your opinion or your view is as valid as anyone else's in the room.

In the fundraising world, charity auctions are made up of items given to organizations by donors or solicited from companies that have a vested interest in that charity. Each charity auction is typically chaired by a group of high-powered men and women who put together the theme for the event, the auction lots, and secure the honorees for the event. In my first decade as a charity auctioneer, I would attend the kickoff meetings or phone call with the event chairs and the rest of the committee as they started to plan their first auction. Despite having hundreds of auctions under my belt only a few years into my charity auctioneering career, I never spoke up when the group would decide that the auction should take place after dessert. Trust me, it wasn't that I didn't know that was the wrong time to place an auction; I had taken hundreds of auctions in front of a half-empty room because the auction was too late in the evening. So why didn't I speak up? Why? Because I mistakenly believed that my voice and my opinion mattered less than everyone else on the call. Because I was younger? Perhaps. Because I am a woman? More likely.

Week after week I would sit in meetings with different committees, some of whom were in charge of their first auction ever, and remain quiet even though I knew from thousands of hours of experience that they were wrong, and I was the one who paid the price onstage auctioneering to a deserted room. And then they paid the price because we left so much money on the table. The definition of a lose-lose scenario.

A decade into my charity auctioneering career I was sitting in my office on a conference call with the event committee and chairs discussing their upcoming gala and live auction. A year prior I had served as the auctioneer for the inaugural gala for the same non-profit held in the stunning ballroom at the Plaza Hotel. The Plaza Hotel's imposing facade can be seen from a cab as you drive down Fifth Avenue. It's been featured in too many iconic NYC movies to name, and walking up the steps of the red carpet through the front doors for a black-tie event makes you feel like you *have* stumbled onto the set of a movie. As you make your way past the elegant Palm Court, where tourists and New Yorkers enjoy evening cocktails at the bar, you walk to the back of the hotel where you are presented with two options to go to the festivities upstairs: an elevator that feels as old and genteel as the hotel itself or the double-wide marble staircases that look like they have come from the set of *Titanic*. I almost always opt for the stairs so I can people-watch the women wearing beautiful gowns, the backs of which spill over the steps, accompanied by gentlemen wearing black tie.

The evening of that inaugural gala, as I walked through the cocktail hour into the main ballroom for a quick sound check, I could tell this was going to be the event of the season. The ballroom was resplendent with gold lighting illuminating the huge columns that supported the arched entryways on every side of the room. Tables cloaked in various shades of gold with oversized flower arrangements in fall colors adorned every table.

While the atmosphere inside the ballroom was warm and cozy, the weather outside was not cooperating. I had arrived with plenty of time to spare for last-minute preparations, which came in handy as I had to make a quick trip to the bathroom to dry the back of my dress using the hand warmer. Rain was sheeting down in every direction, making it impossible to stay dry no matter how you positioned your umbrella. As guests were encouraged to move to dinner by waiters using xylophones, I could tell that the room had lost a number of guests because of the weather. Over the course of the long evening, I sat at one of the back tables watching as half of the audience crept out. I couldn't blame them. After all, it was pouring outside, and in New York that means you can't find a cab. It can easily turn a five-minute wait time for an Uber to a forty-minute wait. But as the auctioneer, I felt the knot in my stomach twist a little tighter with every person that snuck by my table. Predictably, by the time the auction took place, half of the room was empty. I didn't need anyone to tell me that the entire thing felt flat, I witnessed every second of it firsthand. In fact, a decade into my career as an auctioneer, I already knew going into auctions which ones would be successful simply because of the timing of the auction, yet anytime I voiced that opinion and was challenged, I would immediately back down.

A year after the auction, as I dialed into a call with the same organization to discuss their upcoming gala, the memory of that auction was firmly lodged in my mind. After quick pleasantries, the committee launched into a discussion about the run of show for the evening. For the first time, I didn't feel like listening quietly and agreeing as I had done so many times over the years. I heard the event planner mention the auction should take place after dessert. Perhaps it was the thought of pushing through another low-energy auction in front of a half-empty ballroom that made me finally say what I had been thinking for years: "I think we need to revisit the placement of the auction in your event."

The event planner cut me off almost immediately. "We always do the auction at the end after dessert. It's how we have always done it." I was quiet for a few seconds, willing myself not to succumb to the imposter syndrome that was fighting every word from coming out of my mouth.

"I completely understand that it has always been done that way, but my only goal in getting onstage that evening is to raise as much money for you as possible. That can't be accomplished when the energy of the room is flat because everyone is leaving or looking at their watches wanting to leave." There was silence on the other end of the phone.

Another committee member jumped in. "Well, we *have* always done it that way."

I paused again and took a deep breath. While everything about my people-pleasing self was telling me to stop talking, I willed my-self not to back down. *Slam it down, Lydia*, I thought. "I completely understand your point of view. I am sure that I can find another auctioneer who would be willing to do that; however, if you want me to take your auction, we will need to find an earlier time in the program. I don't take auctions after dessert anymore."

After what felt like an eternity of silence, the chair of the com-mittee finally spoke the words that I deserved to hear: "Well, Lydia is the expert, so it looks like we need to find an earlier time in the program."

Instead of immediately overexplaining and thanking them for making the decision that would ultimately yield a better outcome, I simply said, "Great. I'm glad that works." I muted the phone and stood up, feeling so empowered by that moment, the phrase "Lydia is the expert" ringing in my ears. It was the first of many wins over my imposter syndrome. Each time I spoke up, even when it made me uncomfortable, I got stronger.

And I realized that until I believed in myself, no one else would believe in me. Not only did I need to believe in myself, but I needed to believe in my own voice, my opinion. When I confronted my imposter syndrome directly, I realized no one could make it go away except me. That conversation marked the end of my ever taking an auction after dessert. After that call, I repeated the same line every time and received the same results. I was the expert; I had put in the time and dedicated hundreds of hours to learning the craft so that I could do what I did and do it well. When I finally claimed my confidence, I realized I had always had the power to make that change.

There have been so many times over the course of my career that I have found myself in a similar position. When I knew that my point of view should matter and either the people around me made me feel like it didn't, or I felt like it didn't. When I learned to Slam my imposter syndrome and own my confidence, I finally began to believe in myself.

For many of us, it took a lifetime to learn, so it won't disappear overnight. You will have to consciously fight the desire to take yourself out of the game before it even starts. Possibly many, many times. And you won't stop wondering about who is going to give you your next gold star overnight. But if you practice the Slam when the opportunity presents itself, you will have the tools you need to rid yourself of that kind of thinking. Confidence comes when you Slam that imposter syndrome out of your mind. So, Slam the door on negative thoughts and go after your goals. It's time to make your dreams a reality.

ZIBBY OWENS

Author, Publisher, Podcaster, Mom of four

I still can't call myself an author. Or a CEO. In fact, whenever I type out my bio, I feel like I'm joking and that someone will pull the blanket off and reveal that I'm just making this up as I go along. And yet, it's all true. I've edited two anthologies, written a children's book and a memoir. I'm also running a publishing house, Zibby Books, and have an award-winning podcast called *Moms Don't Have Time to Read Books*, which I have developed into multiple platforms that are now divisions of Zibby Owens Media. But I keep thinking that I'm not *really* doing this. What if someone finds me out!? I'd be worried that I had a serious problem if I hadn't talked to hundreds of authors who felt the same way. On my podcast, I listen to author after author saying they can't call themselves an author because . . . they only wrote one book. Or they only wrote a children's book. Or they don't feel literary enough. It's always something. And I reassure them, empowering them to claim the author mantle. "Why else are you here on my podcast?!" I joke. But when it comes to myself, I'm still hesitant. I've longed to be an author for so many years, so many decades, that now that it's really happening, I can't quite believe it. But here it is. I'm working hard to get past this, but the feelings hover like low clouds on a rainy day, just out of reach.

ALISON WYATT

Cofounder of Female Founder Collective

Interacting with thousands of female founders over the course of a year, I get the great fortune to hear their stories, learn about their illustrious careers, and witness the extraordinary future they're looking to build and the society-shifting problems that they're working every day to solve. But somehow, despite all their accolades, titles, [and] achievements in their career, many somehow doubt their place at the helm of their company, doubt their place in asking for those investment dollars, or doubt their place to ask for more money from their customers. This initially came as a shock to me. From my vantage point, nearly all the women I encounter are more than qualified to win, and it would be an honor to be at a seat across the table from them. Instead of these women downplaying the reasons they have made it to where they are or found certain successes, I would love to see a world where they learn to shut off the question that is inevitably playing in their mind of "Do I belong here?"

I want them to ask themselves, "Who deserves to be in this with me?" And if other people make you feel like you don't belong, well, it is my strong opinion that you sprint in the other direction and find a group that not only inspires you but also supports and helps instill that feeling that you have every right to be at that table.

5

GET COMFORTABLE
GETTING UNCOMFORTABLE

What comes to mind when you think of the word "comfortable"? Sinking into a lovely, thick comforter with big, fluffy pillows to match? A warm blanket in front of a fire on a cold winter's day or luxuriating in a hot bath with a good book? In life, we are taught that we should aspire to be comfortable: comfortable in our clothes, comfortable in our home, and comfortable in our own skin. But in truth, it's when we are *un*comfortable, when we are in a situation or a place that feels unfamiliar and uncertain that we learn the most. It's when we are *out* of our comfort zone that we learn the greatest lesson possible: in order to truly claim our confidence, we need to get comfortable with the uncomfortable.

We are challenged in small ways every single day. Every time we are tested, when we overcome adversity, or experience a setback we have the opportunity to grow and learn from it. Every situation that forces us to face a fear or presents us with a new obstacle teaches us

very little about the country aside from what I knew from watching movies and reading the newspaper. I had never in a million years thought that there might be an opportunity for me to visit, let alone an opportunity to take an auction in Saudi Arabia.

My colleague reassured me that they knew I was a woman. In fact, the new prince was focused on empowering women and was very excited that the auctioneer was a woman. He informed me there had been multiple conversations with our global security team about my safety, but as long as I kept a low profile, I would be okay. It was not exactly the most reassuring thing I have ever heard, but if they were okay with it, I surmised, I would be too.

Over the course of the next month, I was so busy with work, the book tour, my kids, and charity auctioneering, I scarcely had time to think about the trip to Saudi Arabia. When it did come to mind, I would immediately force myself to think of something else, to suppress any fear I had about traveling to a region of the world that, from my point of view, did not seem eager to embrace an author who had just published a book about empowering women. The only time I really thought about it was at 3:00 a.m., when I would wake up with a nervous knot in my stomach. I did what I always do with middle of the night fear. I wrote down the thoughts, the worry, the concerns. I got them out. I didn't let them sit in my head and allow the fear to spiral. But most nights when I wrote them down, I lamented my decision to go. It didn't help that almost everyone I told about my trip reacted similarly: "Why on earth are you going there? Is it safe?"

In the light of day, I could talk myself out of that fear. This could be a once-in-a-lifetime experience. Life is an adventure or nothing at all. So, every time I opened an email to try to back out of it, I would delete the email instead of sending it. If you aren't scared, are you really trying? But this seemed like more than just being scared; I was terrified of the unknown. I wasn't only intimidated by the thought of taking the stage in a foreign country where I didn't know the language or, in most cases, how to correctly pronounce many of the artists in the auction. But truthfully, I feared for my physical safety. Yet as the trip approached, my fear mingled with enthusiasm. To keep from backing out, I told everyone I knew that I was going. One thing was certain, if you crossed my path in the weeks leading up to the trip, you knew that I was headed for the Middle East. If I talked about it enough, I wouldn't be able to back out.

As the week of my trip approached, I took a crash course in Arabic from a colleague who spoke the language, intent on learning as much as I could in the shortest time possible to prepare for the auction. But there was also another issue. I am used to taking auctions onstage dressed in cocktail dresses, accessorized with oversized earrings. My outfits are part of my auctioneering persona, a costume that helps me feel like the most confident version of myself. What was I going to wear? I wanted to be able to do my job while respecting the culture where I would be a guest, yet how was I supposed to feel that same energy when I was completely covered? No one seemed to be able to give guidance on what I should wear for the auction except for a fellow female auctioneer who had taken an auction in Saudi Arabia a decade earlier. For that auction, there were only women in the room, so she had felt comfortable uncovering during the event, but since the auction I was taking was for both men and women, I was pretty sure the same rules didn't apply. Looking to the internet did not assuage my fears either. The only articles I could find for foreign travelers to the region were about religious police cracking down on women who showed their hair in public.

Nevertheless, I had agreed to take the auction and there was no backing down. I came up with a solution at the last minute, and that is how I found myself standing at the Saudia Airlines counter at noon on a beautiful, warm June day, handing my passport to the attendant at the check-in desk for a three-day trip to Jeddah, Saudi Arabia. The process seemed to take forever as the attendant flipped back and forth through my passport while I surreptitiously checked out the other women in line behind me. I immediately noticed that all the other women in the queue were dressed in traditional abayas—long gowns that covered their arms to the wrists and their ankles to the floor. I too was wearing a long dress that a friend had lent me. It fell to the floor and covered my wrists, but as I looked at the women in line, I felt self-conscious that my dress was a touch formfitting.

It was, in fact, a touch formfitting. Two days before the trip, one of my colleagues in the Middle East had put me in touch with a Saudi friend who lived in New York. She kindly offered to lend me a few of her abayas for the trip. I was elated—until they arrived the evening before I left for Jeddah. I tried on the first one and laughed out loud. Clearly, the one thing that we hadn't discussed in our far-reaching conversation about Saudi Arabia was height. Judging by the length of the gown, she was probably five foot two, while I am five eleven, which meant that I was wearing an abaya that was better suited for my seven-year-old daughter. Since it was the night before my trip, I didn't have time to buy one, so I threw one over my dress for the journey and hoped that the fact that I was wearing an abaya that also fit my seven-year-old daughter wouldn't be cause for concern when I arrived in Jeddah twelve hours later.

Turns out that was the least of my worries.

After what seemed like twenty minutes of typing on her computer, flipping through my passport multiple times and calling over her supervisor, the check-in attendant looked up from my passport and asked, "Where is your visa?"

I stared at her blankly.

My visa?

My visa for Saudi Arabia?

Yes.

It did ring a bell . . . but not because I had one.

It rang a bell because suddenly I recalled an email from our Dubai office weeks before mentioning something about a visa invitation letter. The letter was in Arabic. I had assumed that it *was* the visa. I pulled it up and handed her my phone.

From the look of doubt in her eyes I could tell that the letter on my email wasn't exactly what she was looking for. I could feel the heat rising underneath the multiple layers of clothing I was wearing as I desperately tried to think of anything that might help me get on an international flight to the Middle East without a visa.

"I am taking an auction for the Ministry of Culture and Information for the Saudi government, so they must know that I am coming,"

I started. I paused, realizing how ridiculous I sounded as I uttered the following: "I am sure it will be fine when I get there."

I should note that I was not, in fact, sure that it would be fine if I ever got there. Truth be told, I had no idea what I was getting myself into at all.

But all of a sudden, the thought of not going seemed like the worst possible outcome to this already bad scenario.

She stared at me. "Ma'am, no one will let you on an airplane to Saudi Arabia without a visa."

"Right," I said slowly, a smile frozen on my face. I realized the futility of my situation, but I also was not willing to relent until I had asked every possible way. "But I have this letter, so . . ." I trailed off. "Is it possible to get a visa today?"

She laughed out loud. "It takes three weeks, minimum."

I am not entirely sure that I heard anything after the words "three weeks." My mind had already gone into overdrive trying to figure out a solution to an impossible situation. She handed back my passport with the firm look of a flight attendant who has been trained to keep delivering the answer "no" as many times as necessary until the person across the counter finally understands that "No" *means* "No."

I turned around and raced through the airport and down the stairs to the taxi line—narrowly avoiding knocking down numerous people—trying to make it up the stairs.

As I snaked through the taxi line, I made a series of calls in rapid succession: the head of our Dubai office, the gallery owner in Saudi Arabia who was organizing the auction, a friend I knew who traveled all over the world. My friend mentioned he knew of an expediting service who could turn around a visa in two hours. I would try anything and everything I could do to make the last flight to Jeddah. The last possible flight I could take was at 8:00 p.m. that evening.

It was 1:30 p.m.

Mercifully the taxi line moved quickly, and within minutes I was in a cab. "Please take me to the Saudi embassy," I asked the driver, dragging my luggage in on top of me.

As I sat in the back of the cab, peeling off the abaya that was stuck to my body, my hands shook. My friend had already texted back the number of his service with a "good luck." I called the number and blurted out my story, ending with ". . . and I am on my way to the embassy now."

The woman on the line responded immediately. "Send me the letter that you showed the airline attendant, and I will have someone translate it and get right back to you." I hung up, not knowing what to do now that the fate of the trip lay in the hands of a service I had never even known existed until two minutes prior. The phone rang five minutes later, and I picked up, praying that she would have good news for me.

I could tell by the tone of her voice that the news wasn't good. "I'm sorry to tell you this, but you are looking at a three-day turn-around, minimum, to get a visa for Saudi Arabia. No need to go to the embassy. This is an impossible ask. You might as well just go home."

Tears pricked my eyes as I hung up the call. Until that moment I am not sure I realized how much I wanted to be on that flight, to experience this culture firsthand and see Saudi Arabia for myself, but also to face the fear I had and take an auction anywhere, on any stage, anywhere in the world. I leaned forward and dejectedly gave the driver my home address.

And just like that, the nerves were replaced with a searing sense of regret. I felt I was not only missing the opportunity to travel to Saudi Arabia, but also letting down my company. In addition, I had also let down the Ministry of Culture and Information, which had been actively promoting the fact that they were bringing a female auctioneer to the region.

As I unlocked the door to my apartment and rolled my suitcase down the hallway to our bedroom, I felt nothing but disappointment. In myself. When things go wrong in life it is easy to pass blame to other people, to make excuses for things you were supposed to do but didn't. To claim your confidence, you have to realize that you are responsible for every decision in your life, both good and bad. I had no one to blame but myself. All the months of precariously juggling the schedules of my family, my job, the book tour, and my charity auctioneering schedule meant that I had taken on too much, and I had finally let the ball drop. I had made a careless mistake that would have huge ramifications career-wise. It felt, in a word, awful. But the mistake was all mine to claim.

I was so absorbed in my thoughts that I didn't notice my phone vibrating until it fell off the top of the suitcase onto the floor. I picked it up; two missed calls from the head of our Dubai office.

This won't be a fun call, I thought, as I dialed the number for the office.

The head of our Dubai office picked up on the first ring. "Lydia. Lydia. Can you hear me? I just got off the phone with the event organizers. They spoke to the embassy. Can you be at the Saudi Embassy in forty-five minutes? They close in an hour, but if you can get there, they can process your paperwork before they close, and you can get on the last flight out."

No thought, all gut.

"YES!" I yelled into my phone. YES. I WILL GET THERE!!

I hung up and looked at my phone. There was no way that I could make it in forty-five minutes. No way. But how could I not try? How could I not even attempt to make it?

There are moments in life where we can choose to stay put in the safety of our surroundings or to go for it. A moment where you can choose to stay or go. Even if the odds are stacked against you. GO! Every. Single. Time.

There was only one thing to do: run.

In traffic, it could take an hour at this time of day, so I sprinted to the nearest subway. Anyone walking down the street in New York would have thought I had lost my mind. Floor-length dress, ninety-degree heat, full sprint.

I was NOT going to squander this opportunity.

I arrived at the embassy twenty-six minutes later, drenched and completely out of breath. I practically threw my belongings into a bin at the security checkpoint, leaving my purse and phone with the security team as I ran to the elevator.

I dashed into the embassy expecting a line snaking out the door, only to find I was the only one there. The man behind the counter looked at me: "Mrs. Fenet? We have been expecting you." I stared at him in disbelief and then burst into tears, overwhelmed by the roller coaster of nerves. I couldn't believe that I had made it in time. I couldn't believe this turn of fortune.

I looked at the clock—ten minutes to 4:00 p.m. I still had time to go home, see the kids, and make it to the airport for my 8:00 p.m. flight. I slumped in the chair, exhausted from the events of the morning. I put my head back and closed my eyes. "Mrs. Fenet?" I looked up and saw the gentleman standing at the desk, holding my passport. "The only thing we need is your ticket information."

You might remember that I left all my earthly possessions with security. You might also remember that I had missed my flight. I hadn't booked another flight, unsure of whether or not I would actually be able to make the last flight out that afternoon. I smiled. "I left my phone downstairs with security—can I forward you the information as soon as I get down there?"

Five minutes later I had booked a roundtrip ticket to Saudi Arabia on Expedia and walked out of the embassy with a brand-new visa to Saudi Arabia firmly in my pocket. I picked up my suitcase, gave my surprised kids one last hug, and was back in a cab headed out to JFK by 5:15 p.m.

I boarded the flight to Paris on time and spent the overnight reviewing the auction lots for the upcoming auction. After a quick layover, I boarded the flight to Jeddah. Then the nerves that had been completely usurped by adrenaline from the "almost missed my flight and lost my job" experience came back in full force. It didn't help that I was sitting in a virtually empty business cabin that felt like it was built around the same time that the Orville brothers were launching their first flight.

I was too wired with adrenaline to sleep, so I sat with my head pressed against the window, thinking about what I was going to experience. After a few hours I could feel heat radiating through the windowpane. I pressed my head against the window, staring out into the vast dark blue of the Mediterranean. The sea changed quickly from deep, dark blue into a turquoise that rimmed the edge of a vast reddish-brown land like I had never seen. As we flew farther into the desert, tiny specks of civilization would come and go. Blink and you miss it. Before long, even those pockets disappeared, and I could see the ripples of dunes that stretched as far as the eye could see.

As the sun began to set over the desert, a bell rang indicating that we were entering Saudi airspace. Another female colleague had mentioned that when you enter Saudi, all women have to change into their abayas and cover their heads in accordance with the local laws. With all the excitement of the trip, I had almost forgotten the other part, the part about going to a country where being a powerful woman was not thought of as a positive.

And there it was again. That familiar feeling. Fear and discomfort in the pit of my stomach about what was in front of me. And yet, I knew this was an opportunity for growth, an opportunity to push through that fear and see with my own eyes what this was all about. The only way through fear is forward. I watched as all the women in the cabin—Saudi and Western women alike—pulled out black abayas that they covered their bodies with and black scarves that they draped over their hair. At that point I only had my short abaya, which

I pulled on over my long dress, and a pashmina that I draped over my head. I had no idea what to expect, no one to ask about the rules that might apply—or not—or anything else for that matter. I knew there was a car waiting at the airport to take me to the hotel, so all I needed to do was get my luggage and head out to the arrivals area. From there I would meet with a small team from Christie's and the owner of the gallery who was responsible for putting together the charity auction.

As I disembarked the plane, I felt like I was in a different world. Making my way through immigration, I noticed that the only women I saw were completely covered in black abayas, head to toe except for a small opening where you could see their eyes. At the front of the line where they were checking passports, the woman behind the counter motioned for me to put my hand on a scanner, to get my fingerprints. I knew I was nervous, but it was clear at that point how nervous I really was—my hand was visibly shaking as I placed my fingers on the machine.

I cleared customs and headed to baggage claim, taking time to look around the slightly dingy airport. Despite the fact that it was almost midnight, the baggage claim area was completely packed with families: fully covered women, and men wearing ankle-length flowing white robes—a traditional Saudi dress called a thobe. I wasn't entirely sure how to act, so I looked down at the ground and walked quickly to the baggage claim to wait for my bag. As the bags started to come out, my phone rang.

It was the driver of my car. "I don't speak English. I drive the car. I'm outside."

I began to explain I was still waiting for my bag, but he had already hung up. It was at that point that the baggage carousel came to a full stop. My bag wasn't on it.

If I had been in any other country, after twelve hours of travel and waiting twenty-five minutes at a baggage carousel, I would have been first in line at the airline counter. But I was unsure what I was allowed to do as a woman. I waited another ten minutes, praying the belt would start up again, before walking over to the claims counter. Then I stood off to the side for a few more minutes before getting enough courage to walk up to the counter.

"My bag didn't make it," I said to the man standing behind what appeared to be the baggage claim help desk.

He looked at me. "Go wait more."

Heart pounding, I ran back over and waited for another fifteen minutes. Even though the baggage carousel wasn't on. It didn't move. My phone rang. It was the driver again.

"I leave?" he asked.

I felt physically sick. My phone was almost out of battery, my charger was in my missing suitcase, I didn't have a change of clothes for the auction, anything to sleep in, or makeup, and the thought of losing the one person who knew where I was going made me feel like breaking down.

"NO. NO. PLEASE DON'T LEAVE," I practically shouted into the phone.

Panic rising on all fronts, I walked quickly back to the baggage claim counter and handed the same man my claim ticket. "My bag isn't here. I've waited for thirty minutes, and the bag isn't here," I said shakily.

He looked at the ticket and looked up. "Your bag isn't coming." My heart sank. "If it isn't here, it must be stuck in Paris, which means it won't get her until tomorrow night at the earliest."

I stared at him in disbelief, tears welling up in my eyes. "But I . . . have an auction tomorrow night . . . or tonight," I said, unsure of which day it was or what time of what day. "Everything I have is in that bag. Everything." The insanity of the past day hit me like a freight train, and I stood in front of him with tears streaming down my face. He looked at me for a moment and then ushered me to the side.

My phone rang, again. It was the driver, again. In that moment all I wanted was for someone else to solve this problem. But getting comfortable with the uncomfortable means you are in charge of the decisions you make at every moment.

When you are far outside your comfort zone, that's when you learn to trust yourself. When nothing seems to be going your way is when you need to dig deep, find the confidence to trust yourself, and figure it out. This is what all the small moments of discomfort build toward: your ability to navigate through difficult circumstances.

It was time to push myself out of a place where everything was going wrong and into a place where I could make things go right. It was time for the kind of pep talk you would expect a coach to give on the sidelines when you aren't pulling your weight in a game. "Pull yourself together, Lydia. Stop crying and go get in the car to the hotel. There's no bag. You have no clothes. But there are places to buy clothes in Jeddah and you can buy something before the auction tomorrow night." I turned back to the man at the counter and handed him my baggage claim. "I fly out tomorrow morning at 5:00 a.m. Can you hold my bag until I get back?" He barely looked at me. I was pretty sure I would never see that bag again.

I walked through the airport and out into the area where the driver from the hotel waited with my name on a placard. "Bag?" he gestured.

"Don't ask," I said.

The heat from outside hit me like an oven. Even at 12:45 a.m., in the middle of the night, the heat was searing, the temperature well above 100 degrees, and the pashmina draped over my head made it seem like it was twice that hot. Despite the late hour there were people everywhere. As we drove down pristine streets lined with the kind of luxury designer stores that line Fifth Avenue or Knightsbridge in London, I looked out at this new country. Aside from the signs in Arabic, I could have been in any city in the US. The only difference was the women who were mostly dressed in abayas as they walked down the sidewalks.

I arrived at my hotel shortly before 1:00 a.m. I had a message upon check-in from my colleagues saying that they were at the restaurant upstairs finishing dinner with the gallery owner and potential buyers. I was exhausted, but I threw cold water on my face and went upstairs to see them. As I walked into the restaurant, I had no idea what to expect. Everything I had heard about Saudi Arabian culture was that men and women remained separated, but here women and men sat side by side.

Immediately, I was embraced by my Middle Eastern colleagues. When I expressed my surprise at the mixture of men and women, they explained that Jeddah was a port city. It had been exposed to different cultures because of travelers coming through throughout its existence. There had also been an edict passed only weeks before that headdresses were no longer needed by women traveling to the country. It was exactly the opposite of what I thought I would see when I walked into the restaurant. It reminded me about one of the most important parts of travel: seeing different cultures with your own eyes. To make decisions based on your experience, not based on the opinions and ideas of other people.

I could barely keep my eyes open as we ran through the agenda for the following day. As we left dinner around 1:30 a.m., the gallery owner organizing the auction asked what time I would be available for the auction that night. "Well, I'm only here for the auction, so you tell me what time works for you. The only thing that I will need to do is find a store, so I have something to wear."

He stared at me. "That will be a problem. Nothing here opens until late afternoon because of the heat." I looked at him quizzically. "The entire city opens up at night because it is too hot to be out during the day. The stores won't be open until the auction starts." Well, that certainly explained the traffic jam at one o'clock in the morning.

He shook his head. "We'll have to open a store early for you."

Be still my heart.

I barely slept that night, my body exhausted but my mind in overdrive about the events of the day and the auction that night. I met with the team the next morning. In the afternoon, my colleagues and I went to a store filled with abayas in every color of the rainbow. As a Western woman, I was allowed to wear the abaya without the traditional head covering, so I picked out a beautiful maroon robe which I wore over the dress I had worn on the plane.

Late that afternoon, we drove out of the newer part of the city to the historic area, known as al-Balad, where the auction was taking place. The royal family would be attending, so security was everywhere. It was definitely the first time I walked into an auction past men with submachine guns guarding every entrance. My nerves were at an all-time high, not only from security—I was also concerned that my commanding style of auctioneering, as a woman, would be considered offensive, or that I might say the wrong thing. Still, the very reason that I had been asked to take the auction in the first place was because of my style, and now was not the time to back down or do something different, no matter where I was taking the auction.

I got up to the podium with a bright smile that belied my anxiety and the amount of perspiration from wearing not only a long dress, but also a robe on top of it. I slammed the gavel down so hard I felt the impact all the way up my arm, my nerves channeled into the smack of the gavel hitting the podium. I looked up, smiled, and launched into the auction with the same confidence I would have shown on any stage in the US. True to form, the crowd responded in exactly the same way. People are people. Emotion is emotion. A bright smile and a little charm goes a long way no matter where you are in the world.

It was the first charity auction ever held in Jeddah, and it raised over one million dollars to support underprivileged children in the area. Half of the auction guests were women, and after the auction I spent almost an hour talking to many of them about being an auctioneer. The conversations were the same conversations I have had with women after I get offstage anywhere in the world. They asked questions about auctioneering, my book, and how I learned to speak in public. As we left the auction, I thought about my preconceived ideas about this foreign country where I had incorrectly assumed that the questions would have been different. More so, that the people would be different. The trip showed me, yet again, that we are all the same. The same fears, the same curiosities, the same questions about power, confidence, and believing in ourselves.

After a celebratory dinner, I left from the hotel to go to the airport. I had gotten very little sleep the night before but wanted to arrive with plenty of time to track down my missing bag. I checked in for my flight at 2:00 a.m. and spoke with a representative from the airport and mentioned my bag hadn't arrived from Paris the day before. He promised to investigate the matter. As I walked through the extensive security check, I marveled at how different it felt to be in the airport now that I felt comfortable in this country. I was no longer nervous. Women in abayas and men in traditional Saudi dress no longer looked intimidating, but rather like the new friends whom I had sat next to at dinner following the auction. The other side of uncomfortable, it turned out, felt normal.

An hour later the flight representative I had spoken with appeared next to me with my missing bag. In addition to the bag, he held up an upgrade to a private suite on the airplane as an apology.

"Feel free to misplace my bag anytime you like," I said as I shook my head in disbelief.

The sun was rising over the desert as the flight took off from Jeddah. I could barely keep my eyes open, but I couldn't believe how different I felt. It seemed impossible to believe how much had happened since I left New York only two days prior. I felt like I was leaving a changed person after such a short time away from my usual life. In such a short time I saw so much, learned so much, and gained so much confidence in my ability to roll with the punches no matter what was coming at me. No auction has ever seemed quite as intimidating since that trip.

You don't need to go to a far-flung country like Saudi Arabia to get uncomfortable in life, though I hope you will have the chance to visit one day. Going to any neighborhood, town, or city where things are done differently, or people see things differently, will teach you that at the core we are all the same.

The next time you are asked to do something, to go somewhere, to try something new, claim your confidence and go for it. Fortune favors the bold, and the bold don't sit around doing the same thing in the same place their whole life. They experience new cultures, see new places, and form opinions based on what they have learned, not what they have been told. And most importantly, they learn that getting uncomfortable with the comfortable teaches you a life lesson you will never forget: outside of your comfort zone is where you start to really live.

MEENA LAKDAWALA-FLYNN

CFA, Co-Head of Global Private Wealth
Management at Goldman Sachs

Throughout my life and career, I have often attributed my successes to luck and not my own merit. Growing up as a competitive gymnast, I lacked confidence in my training. Fast-forward to my early professional career at Goldman Sachs, I doubted my ability to be an effective leader and put increased pressure on myself to deliver results. Although it took years for me to appreciate, I eventually recognized that while luck is involved, my seat at the table and personal achievements have been a culmination of hard work, perseverance, empathy, and leadership.

Reflecting on these moments, there was one common thread: what has led to my success or my learning from failures was finding the confidence to embrace the uncomfortable. While this is easier said than done, I try to remember these pieces of advice:

- You are in the room for a reason. Success is not an accident. It is earned, and it is intentional. Use your voice to bring different perspectives to the table.

- Be naturally curious. Every interaction is a chance to learn and grow in your seat.

- Recognize the importance of sponsorship. I am forever grateful to those leaders who came before me and pushed me to reach my full potential and find my own confidence. Now, I have the opportunity to pay it forward.

Ultimately, life is a series of challenges strung together, and it is up to us to transform challenges into opportunities and, most importantly, to enjoy the journey.

6

ACTION LEADS TO ACTION

Have you ever looked at a friend, a colleague, or someone on social media who seems to have everything going for them and thought that they must have been born under a lucky star? Doors seem to open for them, job opportunities fall into their lap, the minute they have an idea it becomes a reality and things just always seem to work out for them. I'll let you in on a secret: you were born under exactly the same star. No two lives or life experiences are ever the same, but there is one thing that can be applied to every single one of us: action leads to action.

Said differently, and more simply, if you want something to happen in your life, you and only you will make it happen. This is not to say that every single dream you have will work out in life. Just because you can hold a tune doesn't necessarily mean that you will be the next Madonna. But if you create action in your own life rather than sitting around waiting for someone to hand it to you, you will constantly be moving toward the life you want. This may seem like such simple advice, but you would be surprised at the number of people I have met over the years who seem to believe that success in life will come by standing around asking, "Why not me?" Let me assure you that standing around waiting for good fortune to drop opportunities in your lap will get you one place and get you there quickly: nowhere. If you want something to happen in your life, you need to go out there and get it.

There are two paths that people choose when they are approaching life: the path where they empower themselves to make things happen, or the path that also includes a bench where people can sit on the sidelines as they wonder why other people are succeeding when they are not. If you are currently sitting on the sidelines, it's time to change your story. Fear not, by the end of this chapter you will be ready to go after every opportunity that you see in front of you, with the confidence you need to make it happen.

The first rule of success is there is no magic formula that suddenly makes it happen. You will gain confidence as much from the learning process as the result. Expertise comes from doing something over and over again until you have mastered it—and then continuing to do it because to be the best you can never stop improving. Success takes work. Hard work. And until you shift your thinking and understand that nothing gets handed to you, you will never have the confidence to believe that you can change the trajectory of your life and your "luck" at any point. There is always plenty of room in the extra mile because most people will never take the opportunity to go that far. Be the person who always goes for it, and you will find that you are already succeeding just by showing up and working harder than everyone else.

Although I was aware that this was the case over the course of my career, I never witnessed it as acutely as when I published my first book. In December 2017, shortly after I sold *The Most Powerful Woman in the Room Is You*, I was dodging and weaving through the tourist-packed sidewalks of Rockefeller Center in NYC when I walked straight into an old friend whom I hadn't seen for a few months. Realizing the futility of having a conversation on the sidewalk with throngs of people heading to see the Rockefeller Center Christmas tree, we ducked into the lobby of Christie's to catch up. The only thing on my mind that day was the recent sale of my book and I excitedly told her the news. Her first reaction was a loud shriek, followed by a huge hug, and then she immediately pulled out her phone insisting that we make a reservation for a celebratory dinner the next week.

The following week, I sat in an Uber in the standstill traffic that is the hallmark of New York during the holiday season. Realizing that we were going nowhere fast, I hopped out a few blocks early and enjoyed the stroll through Soho on the crisp winter's night. It was Christmastime in New York City, which is the most magical, wonderful time of the year, unless you are trying to get anywhere in the city by car.

My friend had made a reservation at Balthazar, the grand French bistro that sits in the middle of Soho and is the haunt of many New Yorkers as well as celebrities. There was a long line of people waiting as I made my way into the bustling restaurant resplendent with holiday decorations. There are restaurants in Manhattan and then there are institutions in Manhattan, and Balthazar is definitely the latter. The pitched ceiling with antiqued mirrors on every wall creates a lively atmosphere even if the place is empty, but that evening the restaurant was packed. We took our seats at a banquet in the middle of the restaurant and decided that a glass of champagne was in order to start the evening's festivities and made small talk as we waited for our drinks to arrive at the table. When our champagne arrived, my friend took a quick sip and put down her glass. She looked at me with a serious expression and said, "You know, I've always wanted to write a book."

Whenever someone expresses a dream or shares an idea that seems out of their comfort zone, my first instinct is always to encourage them and say, "You should do it." There are always going to be plenty of people who are ready to tell someone else there is no way they can ever achieve their dreams. There are also people who make it their life's mission to talk other people out of their dreams. "You could never do that" is simply not a phrase you should ever believe if someone else says it to you. Yes, there is always a chance you might not be able to do something, but that doesn't mean that you can't try.

The next time someone in your life opens up to you about their impossible dream, be the person who supports them from the minute they confide in you. Make it your mission to support their dream in whatever way you can so they know there is always someone rooting for them. It doesn't matter how grand the vision. If your friend confides that she wants to build a rocket ship and fly to the moon, be the friend who starts plotting a way to get an audience with Elon Musk and get busy designing your space suit so you can go with her. There will be plenty of people to tell her, "You could never do that!" You should be the person who says, "Why the moon? You could probably go farther!" People make impossible things happen all the time. Sometimes a little encouragement is all someone needs to step out of their comfort zone and spark something truly remarkable.

I benefitted from that type of encouragement in my own writing experience. My friend Mary wrote and sold her book years before I had expressed the same sentiment to her. She gave me a copy of her book proposal, introduced me to her agent, and constantly followed up to make sure I was actively working on it. Without her guidance and friendship, it would have taken me a lot longer to make anything happen. Perhaps I never would have done it at all simply because it felt so daunting to take that first step.

That night as we finished our drink and continued on to dinner, I gave my friend my playbook for writing and selling a book. By the time we finished our entrees I had already forwarded her my proposal, pointed out parts that my agent felt were the most important, and encouraged her to use mine as a template. We decided to walk to another restaurant for dessert, so we could continue talking about her ideas.

My final piece of advice was the same advice I had received from my editor. You have to "find your angle" so that your book stands out in a crowded marketplace and ultimately appeals to a publisher.

I left that evening excited about my own book, but also elated that I had been able to inspire a friend to take this journey too. I set a reminder to mention it to my literary agent the next time we met.

As often happens in the nonstop world of New York, we didn't see each other again for a few months after our dinner. I reached out in early spring to get a date on the calendar, and we finally found time to have lunch. As we walked into the restaurant, we had barely taken our seats before I asked how her book was coming. She looked at me sheepishly and then laughed.

"Honestly, Lydia, I haven't written a single word since we had that conversation last year. It's just too much work." I remember nodding in agreement, but also feeling dismayed.

She wasn't wrong. Writing a book is a lot of work. But just because it is a lot of work didn't mean she couldn't do it or wasn't up for the challenge. I knew that she could have done it if she sat down and started writing. Instead she chose the opposite. She chose to let the opportunity pass her by, not to start down the path that might lead her to finally do what she said she had always wanted to do.

After that conversation I noticed a lack of action in people more frequently than ever. I'm sure it was always there, but that conversation highlighted it in such a stark way that I couldn't overlook it anymore. It wasn't just people who wanted to write a book that didn't follow through after mentioning a goal or a dream. It was pervasive.

I listened to another friend tell me she could never find time to exercise though she wanted it to be a priority in her life. She wanted to get herself back into a place where she felt healthy like she had been before kids. Her opening line was always something like, "You are just Superwoman. You always find time to exercise." She's right about one of those things. I am not Superwoman, but I do always find time to exercise. Now that I have three kids, two jobs, and a book to write, the amount of time I have to exercise looks a lot different than what it did when I was single in my twenties.

I pulled out my phone to show her a ten-minute exercise routine I used to do when the kids were little, work was insane, and time was nonexistent—"It's ten minutes," I said.

She shook her head vehemently. "I just can't find the time." I nodded, but again, ten minutes. I don't care how busy your life is—you can find ten minutes to watch a free influencer on Instagram take you through a few moves. Or take a ten-minute walk from your apartment or house. Or do anything to move your body for ten minutes.

When I returned from a weekend trip with my family that involved a long car trip, a friend who used to travel constantly lamented that she could never, ever be in a car with her child for more than two hours. It just wasn't possible. When I offered to pass along what we used to keep the kids occupied for long road trips—podcasts, music, iPad, books, snacks, repeat—she just shook her head. "No way." And yet every time we came back from a trip, she would repeat the same sentence: "I wish I could do that."

Read this next sentence carefully because if you truly believe it, you will be more successful than most people in life. If you want to be successful, you and only you can make it happen. Success will only happen if you pursue it. If you see something that you want, create a plan and go after it until it happens. If it doesn't, adjust the plan and keep moving forward. From the outside looking in, it may look like I have had nothing but success; trust me when I say there have been twice as many failures as successes in my life.

Here's something I haven't exactly told the world: I submitted another book proposal before the book proposal for this book. It was rejected, so I adjusted my angle and tried again. Before I signed with Simon & Schuster for my first book, I had probably sent my best friend's literary agent ten different ideas for books, none of which were strong enough to warrant her agreeing to represent me. I remember waiting anxiously for the emails in response to my proposals, only to receive an email that said, "You have something here, but this isn't it." Don't get me wrong, those words stung each time, but it didn't mean that I didn't try again. Once again, I learned an important lesson: I can stumble, misstep, and fall flat on my face many times, but I am the only one who can pick myself up, shake off those failures, and keep moving forward. I can talk about doing things endlessly, but it isn't until I take action to make things happen that things will start to change.

The other part of success that you don't realize until you start achieving success is that just because you are successful, it doesn't mean it will last. Success does not immediately generate more success unless you keep innovating. You have to continue to actively seek it out and push yourself into a place where you are ready for opportunity the minute that it comes.

Now that I have let you in on that secret, I hope you are feeling inspired to make things happen in your life. You might feel unsure about where to start and how to take that first step to create the action in your life. I want to share with you a few of my favorite tips that I use whenever I am getting ready for my next step or challenge.

ACTION TIP ONE: A WOMAN MAKES A PLAN

In the words of Maye Musk, one of the most inspirational ladies I have ever met, "A woman makes a plan." In order to move forward, you need to know where you want to land. I like to work in the reverse; let's start by figuring out where you want to go so that you can figure out where to start. I suggest using a pencil and a piece of paper to help sketch out an action plan so you can see it in front of you. That being said, this is your life and your journey, so use anything that helps you visualize your path.

At the bottom of the page I want you to write the answer to two questions:

1. What is my end goal?

This is basic.
When you first read that question, what did your gut tell you?

2. Is there something that happens as a result of you achieving this goal or is this truly the end goal?

Now go to the top of the page.

What is the first step in the journey that will get you from where you are today to that end goal? Just the first step. Not the entire process. The first step. Write down that step and then underneath it write what it will take to complete that step. There should be a large amount of white space between that first step and your end goal— you have the rest of your life to fill it in, so don't focus on that right now. Take a deep breath and accept that the only thing you need to achieve is completing this first goal. People put so much pressure on themselves to figure out their entire life as if they have any ability to predict the curveballs that will be thrown in front of them. Start with the micro and you can build over time. First step. Focus.

When I sit down to do this, I like to visualize a row of dominoes. The first step is the lead domino—once you push it down, each domino falls more easily than the one before, right? Before you know it, you are at the end. When you get overwhelmed, just focus on that one piece in front of you that is stopping everything else from moving. Don't worry about what comes next. Push through that first step and everything else will move more easily from there. When you feel confident that you have worked out what it will take for you to move through the first step, write down the second step. And so on and so forth. You should feel a little better right now, a little less stressed at the thought of hitting that all-encompassing end goal.

I do this exercise regularly whenever I am faced with a big project or a goal that seems unattainable. If it is too scary or too lofty an idea, it makes me feel stuck—both physically and mentally— because trying to figure out every piece seems too overwhelming. It almost feels like a brick wall placed in front of me that keeps everything else from happening.

When the clock struck midnight for January 2020, I had already written out my goals for the new year. At the top of the list in all caps was WRITE YOUR SECOND BOOK. But after the world came to a screeching halt in March 2020, our friends and life scattering like confetti thrown into a fan, I couldn't wrap my head around the idea of sitting in one place and writing out another book. Everything felt so daunting, not to mention there were so many other things, like homeschooling three kids, recovering from Covid, and trying to make sure that my family was safe, that kept me from actually sitting down to craft a proposal for another book.

One afternoon after the kids finished online school and I logged off what seemed like my billionth Zoom call, my husband took our kids to the park. In that moment of quiet downtime, as often happens when I feel ready to start writing, I suddenly felt that spark, that small moment of inspiration that encourages me to run and write down my thoughts so I don't forget. The story always seems to grow from that one seed—even if I revisit it weeks or months later. It was weeks before I saw it again—action leads to action—but it encouraged me to grab a blank piece of paper and start this chapter.

End Goal: Finish and publish a second book on the topic of confidence

What do you want to achieve? Continue to inspire and motivate others through writing books

First step: Write 500 words by the end of the week

How simple, right? Five hundred words. While at that moment it felt inconceivable to write an entire book, surely I could write five hundred words. It was easier to think about writing as I took away the looming goal of an entire book. Five hundred words turned into five thousand words, and within a month I had finished the proposal for the book you are reading. As I write this chapter, I am still using the same goal of five hundred words—this time five hundred words a day—to stay on track for my deadline. Whenever the end goal seems too big, go small. Take micro steps to kick-start your goal and build from there. The white space between your first goal and your end goal is there for a reason. Plot your path in a way that keeps you on track and moving forward without overwhelming you.

ACTION TIP TWO: YOU ARE THE SPARK

The days in lockdown during Covid seemed to run together like Groundhog Day. I was lucky to have a job that allowed me to work remotely and stay safe, but not being out in the world was challenging for an extrovert like me who gains energy from being around other people. To combat the barrage of negativity that came from all news sources, every day I would try to find one thing that resembled a silver lining. Some days that took a little more soul searching than others. On days when I was really struggling to come up with anything positive, I would focus on one thing in particular: reconnecting.

In the stillness of a year not seeing others face-to-face, I started calling old friends, often finding myself talking on the phone with people I hadn't spoken with in years. I wasn't dashing in and out of Ubers or running down to the subway to avoid the snarled traffic in the city, so I had time to do more than text, I had time to sit down and have a conversation without any specific topic in mind.

As we moved further into the year, I started to find a commonality on many of the calls even among my most resilient friends. People were scared: obviously they were most concerned about their health, but as time passed, they were worried about their jobs, their financial security, their safety, their parents, the state of the world, and their kids. For most, the weight of this fear was incapacitating. They truly couldn't see past it or even keep their head above water. This was taking a toll on them physically, but also making it difficult to do their jobs or run their entrepreneurial businesses.

One friend I spoke to during this time has always been a business sounding board for me: she is one of the sharpest, savviest people I know. I often describe her as an evolving entrepreneur, as she never passes up the opportunity to adapt or transform her business model to showcase her myriad talents. Pre-Covid, she was known for her beautiful paintings, but even that business idea quickly turned into a franchise: she collaborated on wallpaper, stationary, hotel décor, and even a pajama company. The sky was the limit for her collaborations. She had become so successful in the past decade that her family relied heavily on the income from the products she created and sold.

When I reconnected with her, she confided in me that she was desperately worried. She felt that her family's financial security was at stake, and she was terrified about what would happen in the next year if things didn't change. Many of the physical stores where she had been selling her paintings were closed and she wasn't getting a lot of new business. The worry had paralyzed her, preventing her from dreaming up new ideas and products, which was markedly different from the usual litany of ideas that seemed to tumble from her mind every time I saw her before the pandemic. At the end of our conversation, she admitted that she was barely sleeping because she was so anxious.

Interestingly, from the outside looking in, very little had changed for her actual business. Yes, the world around her was now different and orders had slowed, but what remained the same was her ability to create the product she was selling. I suggested she stop fast-forwarding to the worst-case scenario and instead focus on a solution that would allow her to act and impact change. She needed to be the catalyst for her business—and think about how she could reach people who used to buy her pieces in stores.

With many people stuck at home during the pandemic, home design and décor was one category where people were still buying. She just needed to remind everyone that she was around and had plenty of inventory that she was ready to ship. I guessed that once she saw movement on that end, and was reassured that there was still demand, it would motivate her to start creating again. She needed to focus on what *she* could control—proactively reaching out to her client list from past years, reminding people of her works, and selling off any inventory that she had in her home at that time.

Talk about lighting a match; our conversation was the spark that started a wildfire. She began watching free videos about how to design and market a flash sale on social media. Soon she was blasting emails to her entire book of clients. Within weeks she had created a huge uptick in sales on her website. By reminding people that she was still creating, she sparked the imagination of her client base. The sales also included a surge of people who had purchased in the past reaching back out to work on new collaborations. When she called me to tell me about a particularly successful flash sale one weekend, gone was the voice of a concerned woman who felt like things were happening to her. Instead, she was in control of her life again, simply by creating action.

Whether you are an entrepreneur, the CEO of your home, an assistant in a new job, or someone who owns your own business, remember: *you* are the spark. Anytime you find yourself in a place where you feel insecure about your finances, creating action will make you feel like you are in control of your life again. If nothing is happening, you have to make it happen.

Good things and opportunity do not just fall into your lap in life, just as a fire does not start without a spark. Business does not happen unless you are making it happen. If you feel stuck in a rut or need a spark to start your fire, ask yourself what you need to do to reignite.

Also, no matter what business you are in, it's beneficial to constantly evaluate whether or not your business is growing to keep up with the fast-paced world. It may be that the service that you provide is not as relevant as it used to be, so make sure you are always thinking about how to evolve your business.

When fear and worry threaten to take the lead and you are obsessing about a worst-case scenario, change your focus. Instead of being frozen and fixated on the end result, kick-start your action with micro steps. Set aside a specific amount of time to engage potential leads. If you work better in larger chunks of time, do a few hours a week, if you are more productive at working in smaller sprints of time, do it for fifteen minutes a day.

Use the tools at your disposal and do your research. Comb through LinkedIn, Instagram, Facebook, TikTok, Weibo—whichever platform you use—and watch what other people are doing to engage people with their content, then develop your own voice. Finding a new client can be accomplished by something as easy as making a connection over LinkedIn, sending an email to everyone in your contact list, or a DM over Instagram. Remember, it's not a client's responsibility to find you. It is your responsibility to find your new client.

Social media can be overwhelming, but it is also a powerful and free way to market your business. So just like our first step in your action plan, you need a first step in your social media plan. I suggest working on one platform and getting really good at it instead of trying to be a master of all platforms and winding up with nothing to show for it. Use the social media platform that works for you, the one that you feel comfortable using and that your target clients currently use.

To get comfortable, watch online videos to show you how to use the features that seem difficult. If you feel unsure of how to use it, enroll in a class that will give you easy pointers on how to succeed. If you are looking for a job, this would mean setting aside time to start outreach on LinkedIn. Go through your LinkedIn contacts and see who they are connected to; ask for introductions, ask for email addresses. Tailor each email to the person as much as possible so that it is specific to the person you are addressing instead of something that is clearly a form request. People respond to personal outreach, so whenever possible, make it personal.

ACTION TIP THREE: THE POWER OF SUGGESTION

One of the most important selling skills I have learned onstage is the power of suggestion. Oftentimes when you are trying to sell something to someone, people bring their preconceived idea about what you are selling and how they will use it. If it doesn't align with something that they can see themselves using, chances are you won't nail that sale. This is where the power of suggestion comes in. Instead of thinking about how you might use something, you need to paint the picture of how many different ways this one item can be used. If you have something to sell, write a list of every possible use you can think of, ask a friend what they might use it for, and find new angles whenever you can to help sell the item.

I was recently reviewing the items for an upcoming charity auction. The donor had offered the use of his ski house for a week in Colorado in order to raise money for the nonprofit. When I saw the description, I immediately called and asked if the donor was only offering it during ski season or if the winner could have it for year-round use. I did this because the minute I get onstage with an auction lot that is a ski house, I know I will immediately turn off anyone who doesn't ski. That means that there is zero chance you will continue listening to me onstage. If I am able to get onstage and describe the house as a desirable location year-round, suddenly there are myriad ways the house can be used: a summer getaway for a family to the mountains, a place for people who love to hike and bike, a place for leaf peepers or, if they would rather use it during the winter, a cozy ski house where they can head after a long day on the mountain. Instead of limiting a house to a four-month period for cold-weather adventure seekers, I suddenly have a house that could be used at any time during the year and have opened up my bidder potential to the entire audience. Even if you don't love winter, chances are you love fall, spring, or summer.

The power of suggestion should always be used when you are reaching out to prospective clients. It is not up to them to think of ways that they can use what you are selling, it is up to you to think of all the different ways that they can use your services. Even if they don't employ you at that moment or purchase what you are selling, they might be in a conversation with someone who is looking for that exact skill who could be a potential client. If I want to book more speaking opportunities, I sit down and draft an email to every person I have ever met and remind them that I am a speaker at least every quarter, to update them on any new topics I am speaking on, and to suggest ways in which their company might use a speaker. I use the four seasons of the year as markers for reaching out to potential clients: January—New Year; April—spring cleaning; Summer—slow time, time for learning; Fall—back to school for kids AND adults.

ACTION TIP FOUR: STATE YOUR NEED

Said simply, ask for what you want.

After I published my first book, a number of people reached out to inquire about private coaching. Some were interested in following up on specific elements that I had covered in the book, and others simply wanted to dive more deeply into things they perceived as obstacles they could not overcome with the tools currently in their toolbox.

Although I had never offered my services as a business coach professionally, I had been doing it for years for both friends and acquaintances. I have also been working in business for over two decades, so I was intimately familiar with the issues and questions that most people face in their careers and needed help addressing. And, as you know, when it comes to adding potential revenue streams into my life, the answer is always yes.

One of my first clients was a highly accomplished thirty-year-old who was at a pivotal point in her career. It was clear to me five minutes into our first session that she is a star, an overachiever already receiving the negative feedback that ambitious young women often receive. Most recently, she received feedback that she found particularly upsetting—she was told "she was a little too much."

Interestingly, she felt like this was an insult. To me it meant . . . Watch out world! This woman knows what she wants and isn't afraid to go after it.

She came to the first session armed with an agenda and a list of questions, but I could sense that what she needed was less about business advice and more personal. I was right. We spent her subsequent sessions talking about the negative comments she was hearing, and the criticism and the jealousy she was experiencing from her peers and colleagues for putting herself out there. No matter how confident you are, no one ever likes to hear something negative about themselves.

Sometimes talking to someone who has been around long enough to hear it, handle it, and leave it behind is all you need to know to keep moving forward. And rest assured, anyone who is successful will hear it at some point in their career. The question is whether or not you realize that the talk should inspire you, not diminish you. Make no mistake, the more successful you become, the more people will talk. Just remind yourself that the chatter is likely nothing more than frustration of unfulfilled potential in their own lives. Could have. Should have. Would have . . . but never did.

As we moved deeper into our sessions, we talked more and more about building her confidence Strike Method—her Teflon shield—something she can rely on throughout her career as an ambitious woman. We also spoke in great detail about the importance of surrounding yourself with the right people, but never alienating the people who make the negative comments. Bringing those people into the fold is often the best way to ensure that the talk stops. It's easy to talk about someone you don't know, more difficult when someone goes out of their way to get to know you and empower you to live the life you have always wanted.

During one of our sessions, I could tell there was something that she wanted to discuss but she felt uncomfortable bringing it up. She admitted that she had been asked to do a podcast that she had really enjoyed. She wanted to do more but didn't want to be seen by her internal colleagues as someone who was promoting herself. In addition, she wanted to be a guest on more podcasts but didn't know where to start. I almost laughed out loud.

I introduced her to the phrase that I hope will become your mantra after reading this chapter: "action leads to action." And then I turned the question back on her: "How do you think you can get on more podcasts?" Silence.

"State your need?" I prompted her. "Reach out and ask if you can be a guest on their podcast?"

I saw her eyes widen on the screen. "Do you think I could? What if . . ." she trailed off.

"What if . . . what?" I said.

A reminder to every single one of you. The next time you find yourself wondering "Should I . . . could I . . . ?," remember what I wrote about earlier in the book: no one is handing out a permission slip to live the life that you want to live, to do the things that you want to do, to ask the questions that you want to ask, to go after the dreams that you want to go after. Pull out the piece of paper where you have given yourself permission and then go ahead, ask for it. Go after it. DO IT. And do not look back.

I encouraged her to do just that. To make a list of the top podcasts in her field and reach out to ask if she could join as a guest or offer to get coffee with them to learn more about their podcast, and then they might suggest it to her. I have been on countless podcasts simply because someone sent me an email and, as we know, the answer is always yes. The world that we live in is filled with media companies, podcasts, streaming services who all need one thing: content. If you are an expert in your field or someone who has mastered a certain skill, you should feel comfortable reaching out and letting everyone know you are open to speaking.

In order to set yourself up for success with your asks, spend time listening to different podcasts in your field to understand who the top players are—and then pitch yourself to them with an angle that differentiates you from the other guests they have had on their show. If you don't know how to get in touch with them, the easiest way is to figure out which social media platform they use the most and engage them with a quick message introducing yourself and offering yourself as a guest.

I made these suggestions to my client and a week later I received an email from her that simply said 1 of 5. The first email was titled 1 out of 5 podcasts, the next was 2 out of 5 podcasts . . . until the final email came through that read 5 out of 5. She had reached out cold to five different companies offering herself up as an expert in her field who could speak with them about the podcast. A few weeks later she was a guest on five podcasts simply because she'd stated her need.

I can't promise your attempts will yield success 100 percent of the time, but I assure you that if she had never asked the question, the number of podcasts that she was featured on would be exactly zero.

Over the past two decades of living and working in NYC, I have met some of the most formidable people in the world. And lest you think that formidable people don't have moments of doubt, insecurity, and fear, let me reassure you. They do. Just like you. But what sets them apart is their confidence, confidence in themselves that spurs them to action and pushes them to keep trying when so many other people would simply give up or not try in the first place.

Life is filled with curveballs. But you will claim your confidence when you become the spark and believe that action leads to action. Get ready, because once you have lit the fire, doors begin to fly open, energy comes back to you, and the subsequent actions become not only clear, but often easier. The next time you are wondering why nothing is happening or things aren't working out the way you want, remember that it's up to you. Create your plan, state your need, and remember that you are the answer to everything you want in your life. Action leads to action, so light that fire and get going!

BEATRICE DIXON

CEO and Cofounder of The Honey Pot

When I was fourteen going on fifteen, I told my mother I wanted to get my learner's permit. I went to my mother and told her that this was my goal, because the moment I turned sixteen, I wanted to be able to get my license. My mother looked me in the eye and said, "The only way that I will allow that is if you go to driving school, so baby you are going to have to get a job," and that was the moment my mother turned me into a student of action. She didn't contribute to my driving school because she wanted me to figure it out. I went and happily got a job at McDonald's. Once I got my license, she did the same thing when it came time for me to buy a car. She told me, "I'll pay for half and you pay for half," and that's what we did.

This story has always been important to me because it shows how my mother made me work for everything I had, even though I didn't fully understand how I would make it happen. She never instilled fear in me to go sort myself out. In fact, she made me excited to do it. This has benefited me throughout my life. Whether it was me moving away from home at a young age or me starting my company, she always supported my dreams and made me believe that *I* could make it happen.

Action is the tool that everything and everyone uses in order to move their life forward. I always think of action as my sharpest tool on my tool belt to build the most beautiful life experience possible. I am devoted to my life and purpose on this planet. I choose to be actionable about everything I dream of. I have such a reverence to action that the consciousness, awareness, and respect I have for it almost makes it a religion to me.

I'll end with one of my favorite quotes: "Do or do not. There is no try." Yoda.

7

SAY FAREWELL TO THE MYTH OF WORK/LIFE BALANCE

Whenever I find myself in a conversation about work/life balance, I immediately visualize two scales perfectly balanced side by side. It looks so effortless, so easy for the two scales to remain level, graceful, even. Yet that image always strikes me as a misrepresentation of what balance actually is. Ask a gymnast on a balance beam performing a routine or someone trying to hold a pose during a yoga class: finding balance is neither effortless nor easy. We spend so much time seeking balance that we never stop to think that perhaps the pursuit of the perfect balance is the flaw in this scenario. And if a perfect balance is so difficult, who on earth started the narrative that a balance between work and the day-to-day in our lives is something that we need to achieve? Why do we hold it up like it is the pinnacle of success? Wouldn't it be easier if we could all admit that it is a rare occasion that those scales match evenly, and celebrate those moments as an outlier instead of what we try to achieve on a daily basis? Each of us could likely live a balanced life if we had nothing in our lives that provided any distraction, conflict, or imbalance. But the reality is that most of the time, one of our scales is a little higher than the other one and, for many of us, there are many times a day/week/month/year that one side slams to the floor while the other side gets tossed sky-high. It's time we claim our confidence and stop seeking the perfect balance. Life isn't perfect and balance isn't easy. Free your mind.

I don't remember the first time I heard the phrase "work/life balance," but over the course of my working life, what seemed to begin as a whispered conversation between my girlfriends became a roar heard by every working person in the world. There are now webinars and IG Lives dedicated to telling you how to "strike the perfect balance." There are hundreds of people ready to give you the ten secret steps to take to find balance . . . and they will help you color-code your bookshelf while you are listening to the podcast! It has left us all desperate for the answer to the million-dollar question: How do you reach work/life balance? How can you balance those scales equally? How do you commit as much to your personal life as you do to work and maintain the perfect balance that so many people on social media seem to have perfected and wrapped in a perfectly tied present with a handwritten note?

In short, you don't. I hope you breathed a sigh of relief as you read those words. You can't have the perfect balance because the perfect work/life balance doesn't exist. The next time someone asks you "how do you achieve work/life balance," I hope you walk away.

You will drive yourself crazy believing that there is a one-size-fits-all strategy to help you achieve the elusive work/life balance.

I'm sure your next question is "But why?" Why is there no such thing as work/life balance?

There is no such thing as work/life balance because every single one of us is different. Every single person in this world is on a journey with a particular set of weights on either side of the scales. No two people in this world have been dealt the same deck of cards, are living the same life, or have the same dreams/aspirations. Therefore, the idea that we can all achieve some sort of perfect balance where scales are evenly matched at all times is impossible. Our goals are different, our dreams are different, and the balance between how much we work and life outside of work is up to us and no one else.

Work/life balance is not a static thing. It is the equivalent of trying to drive your car in a straight line on a road that has a million curves. Life isn't linear, it is constantly evolving and changing every single day. The balance of your scales will change all the time. What you need to decide is what it takes for you to be fulfilled in life. Once you figure out what fills you up, you can make changes to either your work or your life, or tweaks to both so you don't constantly feel like you are drained instead of energized. Stop thinking about work or life as separate scales that are perfectly matched. Get comfortable with the idea that the scales are never going to be perfectly matched, that at times the scales are going to be higher on the work side, maybe at times they are a little high on the life side, but the reality is they will constantly be adjusting and correcting.

Ultimately your goal is not a perfect balance, it is making sure you aren't existing in a life where one side is stuck to the bottom while the other side is sky-high for weeks, months, or years on end. Even in the very best of times, those scales will never line up perfectly. So, let's start off by wishing that image farewell.

A large part of living the life that you want to live is drilling down on what is truly important to you and creating a life that makes you feel like you are succeeding the majority of the time. Note that I said the majority of the time, not all the time. Perfection is impossible. Even if you are following someone on social media who appears to have a perfect life, I assure you they have as many ups and downs as you do. Remember that imperfections are what make life interesting. If everything continued flawlessly in your life day after day with no issues and no trials, you would never have a chance to prove to yourself that you are capable of overcoming adversity. Life will throw things in your path that you could never imagine. To keep everything in balance, you need to constantly re-evaluate where you are in your list of priorities so that if you are off-balance you can recalibrate. If you are nodding along with everything I have written so far, desperate to figure out what will make you feel less stressed or stretched so thin you might break, I encourage you to do the following. Find a quiet place and sit down with a piece of paper and a pencil. Writing words on a page connects directly with your heart, unlike typing on a computer, where you are constantly editing your thoughts as you go along. You want your gut reaction to these questions.

Read the questions below and then close your eyes for thirty seconds. When you open them, write down the answers as quickly as they come to you:

What are your three biggest priorities in life?
What actions do you take to honor those priorities?

Your priorities can be anything: family, friends, money, work, travel, health, sports—anything that feels right to you.

To give you an example, my priority list is as follows:

1. To be present with my family and friends
2. Serve others
3. Push myself in my career to provide the life I want for my family

Setting this priority list helps me focus my energy. If I find myself feeling completely out of sorts, or stressed beyond belief, it is usually because I have forgotten to prioritize these things. That's where the second question comes in: How do I honor these priorities in my life? I typically feel most stressed when I am not honoring my first priority—being present with my family and friends. That usually comes because I am taking on way too much without letting anything go. When that starts to happen, I become ruthless with my calendar. If I have a ton of work travel coming up, I sit down and take off anything that doesn't relate to my family. Do I really need to meet someone for coffee in the middle of the day when I am gone on a business trip for two days that week? Maybe. But if it isn't business critical, it can wait. If I don't need to do it, I will push it to a non-travel week or, if I need to go, I am very clear that I have a hard deadline at a certain time.

When I feel like I am having one of those days/weeks/months where the weight of the world is on my shoulders, I think about the second priority. Instead of going to a negative place where I worry about the lack of balance in my life, I stop looking inward. I look outward. I think about ways that I can serve others. A friend tells a story about a difficult time in his life during his divorce, a time when he was feeling incredibly sorry for himself. On a particularly low day he called his mother to vent. His mother listened for a while, but after some time stopped him. She told him he needed to stop complaining and start serving others. He needed to stop looking inward and look outside of himself to help others. His time spent at a local nonprofit changed his perspective and his life. It gave him purpose, a mission, and something else to focus on. You don't have to volunteer at a nonprofit to serve others. Simply connecting with people who are having a hard time, or doing an informational interview with someone, allows you to help someone else. You'll be surprised how it helps you too. If you are in a place where you feel overwhelmed, spend time helping someone else. Connecting with someone outside of your everyday life and, more importantly, helping someone else will refocus your perspective.

When it comes to my third priority, my career, I am always thinking about the next step. How do I grow? When do I hit the accelerator versus enjoying what I have built? Each of these steps plays into my other two priorities. When I was pregnant three times in a little over four years, I realized that if I wanted to be present with my children, those years were not the ones where I was going to be aggressively trying to reach for the next rung in my career ladder. I had spent twelve years relentlessly pursuing the next level in my career; it was time to accept that if I wanted to be present and not completely lose my mind, I needed to look at my career as a marathon, not a flat-out sprint. I had been gunning it in my career for twelve years before I had children. When I was finished having children and felt like it was time to start moving forward again, I was ready to go for it. By understanding and accepting that work and life is a fluid situation, you put less pressure on having it all, all the time.

If I feel stressed about money or work, I sit down and come up with an action plan to address those items. Simply sitting down and refocusing on the things that fill me up immediately makes me feel like I am living a life according to my plan, instead of reacting to things that are coming at me. By removing the white noise and all the extra things I feel like I *should* be doing, as opposed to the things that are priorities in my life, I can move through life feeling balanced instead of out of control. Circumstances can change around me constantly, but as long as I use these three priorities as the prism through which I view all opportunities in my life, I am usually on solid ground.

Another important thing to mentally prepare yourself for when thinking about your work/life balance is that there will always be peaks and valleys. Give yourself a hall pass during the times when you are in a sprint in life or your career. Other things may need to take a back seat for a while until you are on the other side of the sprint period, and that is okay. Use your community and your network liberally and never be afraid to ask for help. Also remember that if you are creating an artificial timeline to get things done, you don't have to do it all exactly when you have written it on your timeline. Timelines are important to keep us on track, but not at the risk of having a mental breakdown.

Once you have your priorities straight, there is another component that will help ensure you feel like you have something akin to balance throughout your life: your ride-or-die support system.

I know, I know, women are supposed to be able to do it all! We should be able to apply makeup like we retain an at-home Glamsquad, bust out dance moves on TikTok like JLo, have children, rock our office job or our job running our home while also making our house Christmas-ready the day after Thanksgiving. But the reality is that if you want to accomplish even half of that list, you will need support. Single, married, with kids, without kids, so many of us try to "do it all" without understanding that what allows you to do it all is asking for help. Trust me when I say that a confident woman who is at the top of her game will tell you that she doesn't do it without asking for help. Every. Single. Day.

I speak from personal experience. Have you ever walked down the jet bridge as you are boarding a plane and seen a mom with a screaming baby and/or a toddler and possibly another child that is hell-bent on running away? The mom is doing a Cirque de Soleil–style contortion act trying to close a stroller with one hand while holding the baby on her hip, using her leg to ward off the jail-break toddler, and balancing bags all over her body? You probably walked by her watching the whole thing with mild curiosity like you might with a crazed animal at the zoo. If you did, by chance, offer to help, she will look back and say, "No! I've got this," with a tight smile that shuts down any further thought about offering help. Well, if this happened five years ago, there is a very real possibility that woman was me. Despite the fact that I would have been fully perspiring from the effort of juggling so many things, as well as being stressed beyond comprehension, I would have flashed you a bright smile as if to say, *I've got this, everyone. Look at me! I can do it all*.

The reality was the exact opposite. Could I do it? OF COURSE. But could I use help? OF COURSE. So why was I refusing help in a situation where I could clearly use it? Because for many years I thought that accepting help was showing that I couldn't do it all. And, as we all know, not being able to do it all is a sign of weakness. Right? Wrong. It's only when you realize that being willing to accept help means you are confident enough to show weakness that you are able to reach your full potential. An additional bonus is you will now have more time in your life to live a more balanced life because you aren't doing things other people can help you accomplish.

My lightning bolt moment came when I was heading home to see my parents while on maternity leave with my third child. I was traveling with three kids—an eight-week-old, a two-year-old, and a three-year-old. My travel hack for traveling with children is to leave an absurd amount of time at the airport. You will never be stressed at a security checkpoint if you have two hours to make it through the line. You can let half of the line go ahead of you and you will still make it to your gate with an hour to spare. There is plenty to occupy kids in the airport, so why make it a stressful experience?

That day we made it through security and were early to the gate, standing first in line as I waited for the announcement about parents traveling with small children. As the gate agent picked up the microphone, he announced a small change; instead of boarding directly onto the plane, we would be taking a bus. Eloise was strapped to my chest in a BabyBjörn, so the only real issue was keeping the older kids from running in front of a moving plane, or so I thought. I immediately started figuring out my new plan. I would simply load our carry-on bags on top of the stroller on the way to the bus, make sure the kids walked in front of the double stroller so they didn't run away, fold the double stroller, load everything onto the bus, and then do it all on the back side when we got to the plane. Easy! As I waited for the agent to finally announce "parents with small children," I felt Eloise squirming and fussing in the BabyBjörn. As she squirmed around, I looked down to calm her just as I realized that there was something wet against my chest. I looked down with dread and realized that Eloise had a massive diaper that had leaked out of the BabyBjörn. Said differently, Eloise and I were both wearing the contents of her diaper. As I looked through my carry-on bag, I quickly realized I had forgotten a change of clothes for Eloise in case something like this happened on the plane. In full triage mode, I excused myself from the front of the line, ran down the hall with all the kids, undressed Eloise, wiped her little body down in the sink with paper towels, rinsed out her outfit in the sink, and half air-dried it as well as her little bum in the air dryer. By that point I had realized that I was getting pretty close to missing the flight. I took a spare nursing blanket, wrapped it between my shirt and the Baby-Björn, and stuck Eloise back in the carrier. My shirt was still dirty, but at least it was covered by the BabyBjörn, and the flight was only three hours, which meant that the only person who would really suffer was anyone sitting next to me on the flight. I half sprinted back to the gate, hauling the kids, the luggage, and the double stroller just as they announced the final boarding call. As I rushed up to the gate, a woman who was also about to board took one look at me and asked the question I was so used to dismissing: "Do you need any help?" Everything in me wanted to assume the "I've got this" stance that I had perfected, but there was no time and YES, I needed help. One minute later, she was helping walk Beatrice and Henry onto the bus and getting them into their seats while the cheerful Delta agent was folding up my stroller and placing my bags into the bus. I looked around in utter astonishment as I stepped on board with a baby in a carrier and a purse. Why had I never asked for help before? Why was I so intent on creating this perception that I could do it all, when doing it all is so much more difficult? My life was so much easier when I accepted help. Help is always there, if you aren't afraid to ask. What had I taken away from myself by allowing someone else to help me in a moment of need?

From that point on, anytime I was boarding a plane, if someone offered to help, I took it. Now that my kids are getting older, I am that mom who walks up to anyone holding a baby/wrangling kids and offers my assistance immediately. I will take your kids to seats, get your luggage into an overhead compartment, and enlist the help of other passengers to help me with all of it. People love to help when called upon. It just takes you asking for that help to unlock that gift anytime you need it. Instead of trying to do it all, ask for help whenever you need it and understand it doesn't diminish the belief that you aren't a capable rock star. In the end, having support will give you the ability to do more. Doing it all takes a tribe, a team of people who surround and support you in good times and in bad times. It doesn't matter if you are single, married, with kids, or somewhere in between, work/life balance becomes more balanced when you are unafraid to involve others as part of your journey.

I like to visualize a strong support system like scaffolding around a building. On the days that you feel like falling over, that system keeps you upright, holds you up, supports you. The most successful people I know are surrounded by people who lift them up and hold them in place no matter what outside forces try to intervene. You do the work to build up your internal self to be strong, positive, and confident, but you build an extra layer of support around you on the days when you need help.

When I think about success in my own life, I think about the community that makes success possible; it's possible because of an amazing support system from my family, my friends, and my colleagues—not only asking for help when I need it, but also taking it whenever they offer. But keep in mind that support is a two-way street. It doesn't have to be returned in the same way it was given, but make sure you aren't always taking over the course of your life. Give freely of your time when you are in a slower period in your life so that others will be happy to help you when you hit a sprint period.

You will have highs and lows in your life, as will the people in your support system. Be sure you are there to help when someone else is having their "mom on a jet bridge moment," no matter what that looks like for them. If a single friend is going through a tough breakup, be the first one there with cookies, ready to listen as they recount every moment of their breakup. If they are having career problems, bring a pencil and paper and start mapping out a strategy for their next move. If a friend is super supportive during a particularly hard moment in my life, I make sure that coffee or lunch is on me the next time we go out. If a colleague covers a meeting when I need to be elsewhere, I make sure that I sit down and spend time listening to them talk about issues that they are facing. I know that people seek out my advice in their careers and I try to be there for them anytime they want to brainstorm business ideas or navigate the constantly evolving work/life balance. Engagement and community make us feel supported in our lives, and you maintain it by enriching and nourishing during both the good times and the bad.

However, the most important place where you need a support structure to help you succeed and feel confident in your work/life balance is your home life. Whatever your life looks like at home—whether you are single, married, a single parent, or undefined—if you are single, everything falls on you, which means that your external support system is even more important. If you are in a relationship, take a long, hard look at your home life and be honest about what you are doing versus what your partner is doing, and what needs to change for you to succeed in your life. One of the most complicated dynamics in a work/life balance is our home life.

As you navigate what it takes to be successful in work/life, one of the crucial elements is ensuring that any partnership in your home is as balanced as possible.

Everyone comes at this conversation from a different starting point based on how we were raised and the example we saw in our own home growing up. I can only write about what I know, acknowledging that every person reading this book will have had a different experience and is having a different experience from mine. I grew up in a very traditional home. My mother is a hyper-accomplished woman who ran a tight ship in our house and excelled in her job as a mom. Because my mother excelled at being 100 percent present, while also dressing us perfectly and keeping our house holiday-ready on every occasion, I used to feel caught between the world that I grew up in and the reality I am creating in my own life. I suspect I am not the only mom working outside of the home, on a different path from her mother, who feels that way. I think it will also be something that every generation deals with as the world evolves. The guilt I felt from not prioritizing my home every minute of the day weighed more heavily after I had children even though I was still working in the office at a relentless pace. It never occurred to me that I should give myself a break; instead I felt like I needed to overcompensate and do everything my mother did. This was also compounded by the fact that it always felt incredibly unnatural to ask my husband to do anything that seemed like my mother would have been responsible for on a daily basis. I always felt like anything having to do with our home should fall on me, as I had seen my mother handle everything on the home front throughout my childhood.

Since my husband grew up in a similar family dynamic, we fell into a similar pattern when we started dating and eventually married.

What I have come to realize, and what I hope you can take away from this chapter, is that the most critical part of being able to navigate a work/life balance is to truly believe and act like you deserve equality in your relationship. This dynamic starts from the earliest days of a relationship with a partner. I can't tell you how many friends I have watched leave their jobs over the years because they started their relationship in a place where the balance was totally skewed from the beginning, becoming further exacerbated when they had children. If you both have demanding careers, conversations about what each person is doing to make your home run smoothly need to start in the early days so that you are setting yourself up for success later. It is critical that you think carefully about what you are doing versus what your partner is doing in a relationship where you are both working. If you don't, you will find that you are doing every single thing in your home in addition to doing everything for your job.

Think about it logically: if you set the precedent in your home for doing everything—buying groceries, laundry, cleaning, cooking, scheduling life, and setting up vacations—while your partner does nothing in the home, imagine what that looks like when you have kids. Now you are doing everything you were doing before and everything that comes with raising a new human being. My advice? Start the dialogue early. Check in often. There is no "right way," but communication is critical to ensuring that you are on the same page of the same book.

I was in the house? No. She was wearing pajamas at 4:00 p.m. But did it matter? No. It was the most freeing moment of my life when I realized that my job is not to treat my partner like another child, it is to expect him to step up like I have when it comes to our life and our children.

I hear so many women say, "Well, my husband/partner/father of my child could never . . ." Of course they can. It may not look exactly the way you want it to look, but that is okay too. So many of us can't get out of our own way when it comes to navigating this crucial piece of life, the piece that gives us the most precious gift of all: time. If you don't think you have to do something, why would you do it? The same goes for your partner. If you are the person saying that your partner isn't capable of doing something, stop making excuses for them, because ultimately it is only going to handicap you in the long run. It's time to get over what you think your relationship "should" look like and make it a relationship that works for both of you, not one of you.

I have recounted the story of my London trip to my guy friends many times over the past few years. I'm not shocked to hear them all laugh sheepishly and admit they don't volunteer unless their wife asks them to do something. It is incredibly frustrating that we are still in a place where the expectation is the woman will shoulder everything in the home life and in the work life. But having those conversations early on in a relationship and every minute after will help set you up for success in your quest for work/life balance. You can't do it all and you shouldn't have to do it all. Two working parents or two working people in a home means two people at home splitting up what it takes to make your home run. It does not mean one person doing everything at home and their job while the other person coasts in and out whenever they want. You are no less deserving of time than your partner, so make sure that you are getting the same amount of time to live and work. If you want to have balance in your life, having a successful partner or support system in life is going to be paramount to you reaching the top of your career. As I said earlier in this chapter, I write this from one perspective. There are many different families, family dynamics, and nuances that will make your story unique to you. If you are divorced, single, a single parent, or any other way of living your life, I can only say that finding your tribe to help you in the moments when you need help is going to be a critical part of your life and ultimately your success in life.

When it comes to work/life balance, stating your priorities and ensuring that those are always front of mind is key. Creating a strong support system both at home and, for those of you in the office, with your colleagues, will give you the confidence to reach higher and higher. Don't expect your life to look the same at every moment. Accept that there will be moments of insanity and there will be moments when it calms down. There are moments when you go all in and there are moments when you can pause and breathe. Wherever you are in your journey, be unafraid to go after everything you want and more. Claim your confidence and surround yourself with people who will be there to cheer you on or cheer you up in equal measure.

EVE RODSKY

New York Times Bestselling Author of *Fair Play* and
the National Bestseller *Find Your Unicorn Space*

Time is our most valuable currency. And yet women are taught from an early age to give theirs away to our partners and our professions, or to magically expand it to fulfill the needs of our children, friends, and family. Because I know this all too well, I believe it's time for a "time revolution," where we reclaim some for ourselves. More time to become curious, to reconnect with a skill, talent, or interest that gives us joy outside of our work, our family, and our other obligations. In our too-busy world, most of us regard time as a nice-to-have, but it is essential if we want to avoid burning out, opting out, stressing our partnerships, and, ultimately, losing ourselves. We can begin to reclaim our time when we give ourselves permission to be unavailable, to set boundaries, to say one beautiful word: *no*. When we can bravely write our own "permission slip" to disengage from all the societal guilt and shame that tells us how we *should* be spending our time, and instead reengage in the active and open pursuits that make us feel most alive, we model an unapologetic openness to women everywhere to become interested in their own lives at any age or stage of the game. I'm not sure where my next "time out" will take me, but what I do know is that I will continue to devote my life to making the world better for the women coming up behind me. To me, this is time well spent.

8

SHARPEN YOUR GREATEST
LEARNING TOOL: FEAR

Do you remember how old you were when you first felt fear? I don't mean a childhood fear like monsters under the bed, a fear of saying the wrong thing to the kid you had a crush on, or wearing the wrong thing to a school dance. I'm talking about the type of fear that is so incapacitating that it stops you in your tracks. The kind of fear that wakes you up in the middle of the night and keeps you awake for a couple of hours as you think about opportunities that passed you by, money, the state of the world, or the health of your family or friends. Do you remember where it started or how, at times, it took hold in such a way that it kept you from trying new things or going after something you really wanted? Can you remember a time in your life when fear didn't play a part in the decisions that you made or opportunities you passed up? Do you wish that you could describe yourself as fearless?

Fear is about confronting the unknown. We fear what we can't see, what we don't know, or haven't yet experienced. No one in life is completely fearless. Confident people understand that even though they are fearful, they can move through that fear and then learn from their experience to help them keep growing. The only way through fear is forward. When you claim your confidence, you will begin to see fear as a tool that can make you stronger. Every time you overcome something that could have stopped you, you grow, which gives you the ability to move past that fear and unlock bigger goals and opportunities.

Fear, especially for women, often comes into sharp focus because of social or cultural forces. As women, we are taught that there is nothing worse than being disliked or being thought of as unlikable. We fear embarrassment—of speaking out of turn, saying the wrong thing, or seeming too forward. Real or imagined, I hear this from even my most fearless friends. We live in a world where women have been told how to act, how to behave, and how to be for most of our lives. But we don't *have* to do any of those things. In fact, the opposite is true. The more we confront the things we fear the most, the more we will learn how to sit with the fear, move through the fear, and stop seeking validation from others, which leads to greater confidence.

Twenty years into a career as a charity auctioneer, I have been asked innumerable times if I am scared before I get onstage. The questions continue from there: "Are you worried that the audience won't listen? That you won't raise enough money? That you'll say something wrong?" In short, of course. The first few years I could barely sleep the night before an auction. I felt like my entire body was on edge as the day progressed, my nervousness intensifying the closer I was to walking onstage.

Over the years I created techniques like the Strike Method or the Slam to overcome this, an act that pushed me from feeling as if I didn't have control to a place where I felt like I *was* in control. But that just helped me get onstage. Every time I walked onto that stage and pushed *past* that fear, past that scared knot in my stomach and the adrenaline that came flooding in, I would walk off the stage feeling twice as confident. My earliest auctions were for smaller groups of people—two hundred to three hundred people in a crowded ballroom—but as I started gaining more experience, the sizes of the auction crowds grew until my normal Tuesday was no longer three hundred people but rather nine hundred people. Each time I pushed myself to take a bigger auction, I received the ultimate reward, more confidence on the other side of fear. While that fear felt almost debilitating when I first began, over time that same fear—the shaking limbs, the uneasiness, the adrenaline flooding into my veins—became energy that I would use to move and energize the crowd. I learned to harness the fear and turn it into a positive.

Fear is a double-edged sword. On one hand, fear can make you complacent when it keeps you from trying, from pushing yourself forward. But when you overcome fear and confront it head-on, not only do you keep moving forward, you get stronger. That's when you gain confidence, when you face fear, feel that fight-or-flight feeling, and you plant your feet and choose to fight. That's when you prove to yourself that you are strong enough to handle anything. Because you are. We all are.

When we look back on 2020, I know we'll remember many moments of fear. But it's inevitable that those moments forced us all to grow in our own way. Without a doubt, the moment when I learned to push through fear happened as it did with most of us, at the beginning of the global pandemic.

Earlier in the summer of 2020, it became increasingly clear that the world's collective hope that the pandemic would be over in a matter of weeks was not a reality. Like everyone else in the early months of the pandemic, Christie's, the company where I worked, was trying hard to keep the business profitable; but no business was untouched during this time. We sell luxury goods. As people became worried that they needed to wipe down groceries to keep from dying from a disease that no one knew how they could get, buying art was not on the top of anyone's list of things to purchase.

New York had essentially shut down in March 2020, which is typically the month that the auction world goes into high gear. This is when Christie's galleries all around the globe are filled to the brim with some of the world's finest art and luxury items. However, with the US and most of the UK/Europe locked down, we weren't able to host the auctions that bring in a sizeable amount of profit. This meant that there was no possible way the company could come close to hitting our budget for the year. And it didn't seem likely that people would be flocking to crowded auction rooms packed with bidders anytime soon. Having worked in my company for over two decades, including the dark days of the financial crisis in 2008, I knew at some point the decision would be made to start cutting costs. Spoiler alert for those of you just starting out in business. When you hear the words "cost cutting," get ready for the next business phrase coming your way, "layoffs."

Having been through many rounds of layoffs in my company over the past twenty years, I am intimately aware of the way the process unfolds. The conversations start at the top of the company a few weeks before anything happens. Usually an executive who is privy to the information swears to secrecy a friend or colleague . . . who invariably mentions it to someone else. Within the next week it seems like everyone knows that layoffs are imminent, and people begin guessing on departmental text chains who will be the first to go, while not so secretly praying it isn't them.

When I ran the special events department, I remember a key indicator of layoffs was a request from a senior administrator asking that the viewing rooms and boardrooms were set aside for a "senior meeting," without specifying what the meeting would cover. One thing is for sure, if you see the name of an HR rep pop up on that day, you might as well pack your office before you leave for the meeting, because that will be your last day as an employee of the company. In short, by the time layoffs finally happened, the rumor mill had given everyone about two weeks to prepare for the inevitable.

Yet once we were all isolated because of Covid, we were relegated to our homes without time for a quick office drop-in or a chance meeting on the street where that information could be passed along. Zoom calls allowed for exactly zero gossip, and so there was no advance notice about impending cost cutting or layoffs. There had been a series of smaller cuts and requests for voluntary pay decreases among the senior executives, but by summer 2020, without a single sale since March, it was clear the company had to act.

As I had seen many times, the dreaded calendar invite sent from our CEO's office arrived in everyone's inbox in the middle of a workday requesting an all-staff meeting the next morning. I don't remember being nervous about layoffs in the past, but now the uncertainty around every aspect of my life made it seem like this could be the year that anything was possible.

As I typed my name into the Webex account the next day, I could feel anxiety coursing through my veins, fear in its purest form. My mind was playing out every possible scenario, including the worst case: the company would close its doors, all departments that hadn't hit their budget would be closed down, my entire team would be fired. I had made it through the 2008 recession by responding to this exact issue, turning my department from a support team into a profitable unit in its own right. This year did not look like it would be our best year, but I told myself we had deals in the pipeline, so we would be safe . . . wouldn't we? The realization that there was a chance that I could not only lose my own job, but also that I might have to lay off my entire team, made me feel positively ill.

As our CEO came on-screen, one look at his face told me all bets were off. Predictably, he told us that without knowing when the art market might rebound, we would need to make extraordinary cuts throughout the company. The next days would be incredibly painful, and he understood that it would be difficult for everyone.

Reorganization was the name of the game, and trusted friends and colleagues would be let go in the coming weeks and months. Throughout the speech my team was texting me:

Are we okay?
Are we going to get fired?
Are they going to shut down our team?

Whenever I am faced with leading in a crisis situation, I always try to think about what I would want from my boss in that moment. For me, the answer is always the same: honesty. Don't sugarcoat, just give it to me straight.

Hey guys, I don't have an answer. I will tell you as soon I
have a better sense of what is going on. I will let you know
the minute I have an answer, I promise.

As our CEO signed off, telling us that our HR reps would be in touch with next steps, a notification popped up on my screen from my boss requesting a meeting fifteen minutes later. I felt a wave of adrenaline course through my body. You know, the one that you feel when you fly by a police car driving ninety in a sixty-miles-per-hour zone and everything in your body goes limp? I stared down at my phone in disbelief for a minute, and then stood up and walked outside.

Whenever I am getting bad news or dealing with an emotion that does not feel positive, I have to move. Moving makes me feel like I am in control; sitting makes me feel like I am at the mercy of something else. Not knowing what else to do, I started to pace back and forth, feeling the fear coursing through my body as tears pricked my eyes.

With fifteen minutes until the meeting, I continued to pace back and forth, breathing deeply and collecting my thoughts. Giving myself the pep talk I knew I was going to need to address the news I was fairly certain was coming, I focused on keeping myself in a position of power, trying to give myself control over a situation in which I felt completely powerless.

Even when you are in a situation that feels out of control, you can *still* reframe it to keep yourself from going to a place where the world feels like it is ending. You can rewrite the rules. For me, that meant staying clear-headed and dealing with the logistics of what would be presented. I *did* feel that the world was ending, so here was what I told myself to reframe as I paced:

Do not cry.

Yes, I tell myself that too.

Keep your composure.

Nothing is gained by losing your temper or losing control.

Write down your questions. Writing things down would allow me to get the details right and refer back to them after the conversation ended.

No matter what happens, you will be okay. You can figure this out. You can and you will. This is a moment in time. It does not define you.

Do not say anything until he's finished talking.

One of the first rules in any negotiation is to let the other person

164

do the talking. And this would be a negotiation even if I was getting fired.

Fifteen minutes later the phone rang. I took a deep breath. "Hello?" When he responded, the tone of his voice was the answer I needed. He didn't even need to continue. I had my answer. A normally enthusiastic, high-energy guy, he sounded completely deflated. We typically spend the first five minutes of calls making small talk about things going on in our lives or in our company— but it was clear that was not going to be the way that this conversation would be taking place.

"You have two options here, Lydia, and neither of them are good," he said. He reiterated that the financial position of the company was dire, and they were going to need to take drastic action to get things under control until we had a better idea of what was going to happen to the art market. "You can either take a severance package or you can take a substantial pay cut and reduce the number of days you work in the office." I felt like I was having an out-of-body experience.

No good options would be accurate, I remember thinking. As he was talking, I fought back tears and tried to remember what I had said to myself during my pep talk earlier. Anytime I felt a lump in my throat or wanted to interrupt to make a point, I remember thinking, *Don't say a word until your voice is strong again.* I wasn't entirely sure that I could hold it together. I asked about the members of my team, who thankfully were still safe at that point, and then hung up by saying I needed time to digest what he had just said.

As I disconnected from the call, I felt sick. There was the obvious problem that I now faced, which was two bad options for my career of twenty years. But there was something I hadn't shared with my boss, which was that my husband had lost his job in April of that year. His company had made cuts as well, which meant that my income was critical for my family. We had savings, so all was not lost, but without any idea how long the pandemic would continue, how long my husband would be unemployed, or whether I would be able to recoup my lost salary, there was one thing I knew for sure: there was no way we would be able to continue to live in New York City if things didn't improve or if I couldn't figure out a way to supplement my income.

I have been on stages and given speeches about women in the workplace around the world. When discussing career obstacles, I am always the first to stress that in business, it isn't personal. There was no question that I was now going to test out that theory firsthand. Still, after two decades in a company, it also felt like the worst kind of betrayal. I felt so many emotions: numbness, fear, sadness, embarrassment, anger—each emotion bubbled up on its own before the next one replaced it. I felt my eyes well with tears and then, predictably, I started to cry.

I always tell my oldest daughter when she gets upset that sadness is an emotion just like happiness. We can only know the highs of happiness if we allow ourselves to feel the lows of sadness, and to *let* ourselves cry, *let* ourselves feel deeply. And cry I did. That moment became the catchall for so many things. I cried for the upheaval in our lives, for the disruption to the city that had been my home for two decades, for the ever-present fear, for the well-being of my friends and my family. And I cried for the loss of stability—all the regularities of life that were now gone—case in point: the security of my job. And I remember thinking to myself, *get it all out now*. Cry, kick something, scream. When something bad happens, something unexpected that could drag you down as far as you let it, you can't deny your initial reactions. The way out of the low is to go through it. For me, this meant indulging my need in that moment for self-pity with a side of sadness.

You can also really let it all out if you know you aren't going to stay there, if you won't sit in that place forever: so, give it a time limit. *You have an hour to get this out of your system, Lydia*, I told myself. *Take the time and wallow in self-pity. And then you need to pull yourself together and come up with a plan.*

What happens when you are faced with something difficult, personally or professionally, something challenging that forces you outside your comfort zone? When your back is against the wall, what do you say to yourself? Do you think about the consequences and fast-forward to the worst possible outcome? Even if it is your initial reaction, I can promise you that to go to the negative is a race to the bottom. So, what is the alternative?

Fight. For yourself. Even when you are not the final decision maker or the person calling the shots, that does not mean the situation is out of your control. It means that you need to reframe it in a way that allows you to *believe* that you are in control of the situation. If you believe you have no control, you are likely to choose the path of least resistance, without taking time to think through options. The way that you respond to something that you think you have no control over can dramatically change the way you feel about yourself, and help you feel confident even when things don't go your way. Do not opt out. Opt in. Believe in yourself even when it feels like others don't believe in you.

I have often said that when I am backed into a corner, I do my best work. But again, it's easy to say something and quite another thing to do it. Having been in situations where others are doubting me many times in my life, one thing I know for sure: Confidence is knowing that no matter how bad things may seem, you do not give up. You do not believe that the whole word is against you. You do not cave in to fear. You realize that things change, plans are disrupted, life is disrupted, but that does not mean you count yourself out. It means you innovate and find a way to continue moving forward. You grow in these moments, and you learn to trust yourself.

When I was done crying, crying, crying and feeling sorry for myself, I put on my running shoes and went for a run. Moving not only helps release endorphins when you need a mental pick-me-up— it also helps you feel unstuck.

As I ran, my boss's words echoed in my head: "You have two options here, Lydia, and neither of them are good." But, I realized, those were the two options that my company had created for me. Just because they thought there were two options didn't mean that there were only two options, it just meant that I had to think of other options. Don't believe that the only version of the world is the one that others see for you. You aren't beholden to the vision or plan that someone else has created. Do not allow others to create a future for you. You create your future.

Confidence is understanding that not everything works out the way we think it will. We need to be able to pivot and be ready to come up with different ideas and plans to help us continue moving toward our goal. Don't look around for someone else to save you. Look within. Everything you need is inside you if you have the confidence to put yourself out there and try.

As I ran, I kept repeating to myself, *Okay, Lydia. What is the third option? What is the third option? What is YOUR third option?*

If I took the package, I would receive severance, which meant I would get paid a sum commensurate with my time spent at the company. All was not lost, but we would lose health benefits as a family and there was no way of knowing how long the pandemic would last, or what would happen to the art market long term. Also, I would be walking out on twenty years of sweat equity and strong internal relationships.

There was also the issue of pride. Twenty years is a good run, and I wasn't about to leave on someone else's terms. At the same time, I couldn't afford to lose so much of my income. How could a pay cut be a positive? What was that third option? *Keep digging,* I thought. *It's there. Keep thinking.* Every footstep gave me more and more clarity. How could I protect what I had built at Christie's, create a revenue stream, and keep my confidence intact?

It was time to practice what I always preach: you are what you negotiate. When I got home from my run, showered and dressed, I wrote out my action plan. First things first, I needed to understand my rights. I called a friend who is a lawyer to speak to her about my options. I know most people would balk at the thought of arguing about something so clear cut, but to me, making sure I am asking and understanding every possible outcome makes me feel like I am leaving no stone unturned. Knowledge is power, so I made sure to ask every single question that came to mind in order to understand every nuance of both "not great" scenarios. After speaking with her, I decided to go back with a counter proposal: I would work four days a week with a slightly smaller pay cut instead of three days a week with a larger pay cut.

Obviously, I wanted them to agree to everything counter-proposed, but as a businesswoman, I also knew that the chances were slim. It was an unprecedented year, and I was certain exceptions would not be made for anyone in the company. As I pushed send on my email I was certain the answer would be no, but at least I had not accepted the news without a fight. When you understand that rejection will not kill you, the word no is simply a word. Once you realize that, you stop fearing it. You can take a risk.

I also kept thinking beyond that possible no—*if* the answer was no, what could I ask for even when I was taking a substantial pay cut? How could I make it work if I wanted to stay? Somewhere between sending the letter back to HR and receiving the final answer from Christie's, it finally came to me. I realized that instead of looking at the pay cut as a loss, I needed to shift my perspective and look at this differently. This loss of revenue would be painful, but it could allow me to gain the most important thing you can have as an entrepreneur, as a businesswoman: time. Part of the pay cut was the potential to work three days instead of five days. If I could gain some of my time back, I could use that to create an external revenue stream to offset the loss of income from my job. That would also allow me to build other business opportunities that could make up for the lost revenue. It would give me time me to write another book, time to come up with new ideas and find new revenue sources that I hadn't yet discovered. My ask would be that the company would allow me to market my side business in the open, in parallel with my job. In time, that business might become big enough for my career to go in an entirely new direction.

I quickly got to work drafting yet another email to my boss. The paralyzing fear that I had felt during our conversation only a few days prior seemed like a distant memory. I wasn't sitting around worrying about what could happen, I was taking steps to make sure that I was in control of what was happening. If they were taking income out of my paycheck, I argued, they had to allow me to use my two days off to make money. When I heard back, as expected, the company didn't budge on their initial offer, but they did agree that I could market my side business. At the final meeting I told my boss one thing: "I believe in myself more than this company or any other company out there." I did, and I do, always. There is no plan B. There is only plan A, and I am plan A. Always.

If you were raised reading nursery stories about princesses saved by a prince, a frog, or whatever magical creature the story chooses to tell you, know this: You don't need anyone else to save you. If you are confident, willing to put in the work, and believe in yourself, you can save yourself. Nothing makes you feel more fearless than knowing that you are in charge of everything that happens to you, good or bad, and that you have the confidence to handle it.

After a few weeks of back-and-forth, we came to a final decision. I would keep my title, work three days a week, and take the pay cut, but I had the company's blessing to actively market any side business on the two days I was not in the office. There was one other thing that I kept in mind throughout these discussions. Even though my boss had been definitive about the fact that there was no plan for me to return to five days a week and a full salary, no one knew what would happen next in the world.

Six months before, we had been having one of our best years ever; six months later, we were having layoffs and salaries were being slashed around the company. Who knew what the next six months would bring? The next year? The next two years? Too often I see people around me take the short view of a long game. They are busy playing checkers while I am playing chess. You need to be thinking eight steps ahead. Life is long; your career is long. Whenever you are panicking about the here and now, remember that life has many ups and downs. You won't win every time, but the point is that you don't walk away from the game unless you have left everything on the floor. Every single time. I made the decision that I would let my work speak for itself, and lobby for my original position when the time was right. Or, by that point, my side business might have completely usurped my job and I would be ready for a change. I wasn't on the back foot anymore, reacting to a worst-case situation by hiding under a blanket. I was facing it head-on and sharpening my greatest learning tool, fear.

While we were finalizing details with HR around my new contract, I was already working full steam ahead trying to figure out how to create an income stream out of thin air. Confidence comes from creating your road map and then carefully plotting to ensure that you are on track to make things happen on your terms. I needed to create a way to make up for the lost income until we had a better understanding of what the future looked like post-pandemic and I needed to do it quickly.

Starting in July 2020, I held two concurrent jobs: overseeing the strategic partnerships team at Christie's, taking almost every virtual charity auction on their behalf, and running my ever-growing side businesses. I created a masterclass online, coached private clients, built my speaking career, worked with a producer to sell my first book to Netflix, and wrote the proposal to sell this book. As my husband looked for a job, he also took over all the financials for my side businesses. The things that I always hated—invoicing, bookkeeping, and contracts—were his forte. I had always joked that we would never be able to work together, but in fact, we made a great team. Since we were both virtual, talking about my business became part of our every day.

Though I took the pay cut at Christie's and worked three days a week, I was still committed to making my department profitable. I had been holding a daily morning meeting for my team that had started in March 2020, and I wanted to attend every meeting that was critical to the success of my department. I found that holding firm to the two days off was difficult.

Soon, though, I found a way to structure time in a more fluid way, so that I could attend meetings on the days when I needed and give speeches, coach private clients, speak on podcasts, etc., when I was off. The knowledge and the contacts gleaned from my masterclass were helpful in my role at Christie's and helped grow my network even further. In addition, the side businesses added a new dimension to my life I relished.

As we entered 2021, I saw that companies and humans craved the connectivity we had been missing and would want it to return as soon as possible. Christie's had moved at light speed to transform from a brick-and-mortar structure where people came to watch auctions into a slick, digitally driven auction room complete with a beautifully created stage and bidding capabilities that far outweighed what had existed only months before. Simultaneously, my side businesses took on a life of their own and filled both of my days off easily. I also realized something else: I enjoyed the side businesses more than the work that I was doing on a daily basis. In time, who knew what could happen? Ultimately, it might be more lucrative to leave rather than stay at the new salary. The world was changing, and what I thought work should look like had changed as well. Regardless of what happened, I would be ready for it. Unafraid. Up for whatever challenge came my way.

The more you face your fears, the more you will learn that even if the worst-case scenario does happen, you will be strong enough to make it through. Each time you overcome, persevere, or survive, you realize that not only can you make it through, but that experience becomes part of the fabric of who you are.

As I write this chapter, we are watching yet another spike of

Covid sweep through the US. Yet instead of witnessing another fear-induced paralysis, I have watched my most cautious friends react with resilience. They have been through it; they know what to expect and they know it will pass. We learn, we grow, we move through fear, and we gain confidence to overcome the next challenge, no matter how much we fear it. The lessons we have learned in the past few years will make us all stronger throughout our lives, capable of handling more and living the lives we deserve. But we have to do the work, to learn to sit with fear and know that it doesn't hold us back; it frees us to reach even greater heights.

RUCHI KOTAHWALA

Creative Director and Founder of Ruchi New York

Fear is the most powerful emotion that holds a person back, preventing one from taking risks and leading to low self-confidence. It primarily stems from two types of things: fear of losing someone/something or fear of being judged. I migrated from India twenty years ago. I was born into a conservative Indian household where women never went to work. Four years ago, I decided to divide my time between my family and work by launching my fine jewelry brand, Ruchi New York. I was daunted by the judgment of relatives, friends, and others that expected me to fit the norm of the conventional stay-at-home woman. Nonetheless, I followed my passion for designing and being an entrepreneur. By being fearless, I was able to do what I love, fulfill my goals, and, as a result, convert those who I thought judged me into my biggest supporters.

I have been designing since I was sixteen; my husband and his family have five generations of legacy in the gem business. I was always at the back end, actively involved with designing and product development. My close friends strongly encouraged me to share my pieces with the world by launching a brand that would be direct to consumer. Initially, they wanted to host a trunk show for me, but I was hesitant. My biggest fear was the fear of rejection. What if nobody showed up? And even if they did, what if they didn't buy anything? Or they didn't like my work? But I overcame these frightening hypotheticals and persisted onward. I decided to do a trunk show to benefit my friends' charity supporting underprivileged women around the world. This was the very first one and I couldn't sleep the night before. Even though I didn't sell much at that particular event, I learned to let go of my fears. I adopted a new philosophy: Do your best and control what you can control and let go of what you can't.

Since then, I have hosted dozens of events, spoken at public and press gatherings, and sold to a plethora of A-list celebrities and several C-suite people of Fortune 500 companies. When you let go of fear and are determined to pursue your dream, opportunities flow in and your inner potential and confidence is revealed.

Even when you are feeling weak in the stomach or wobbly in the legs, all you need to do is stand proudly and reflect an aura of confidence; if you can do this, I am certain that you will attract the best opportunities. The only way to achieve fearlessness is by believing in yourself.

After all, the only thing that fear is afraid of is confidence!!

9

GROW YOUR MINDSET

When I hear the word "growth," I always think of growing upward: a child in the middle of a growth spurt who suddenly finds that her pants are too short, a tree growing so high that it looks like it is trying to reach the sun, or a flower blooming upward out of the ground. But when it comes to growth mindset, the path is far from linear. Having a growth mindset means growing in all directions, of constantly evaluating and reevaluating your surroundings and thinking about how you can explore as many directions as possible.

As I mentioned earlier, when the global pandemic hit our family, my husband lost his job and I took a substantial pay cut. At that point, I knew that I needed to increase my income stream in some of my other businesses. But it was one thing to see an issue in front of you and another thing entirely to address and create growth from that opportunity. And since you are claiming your confidence,

I want to show you what growth mindset looks like on a practical, no-nonsense, "you can do this right now" level so you can apply it to your life starting today.

Let's start with the most important thing that you need to have a growth mindset: a clear picture about what your expenses are in your life. If you are spending without saving or spending without knowing how much you actually have in your bank account, you aren't in control of your life. Understanding what you have is a crucial first step in having a growth mindset because being in control of your financial life is crucial to feeling confident in yourself. When our salaries were reduced, we made sure to match that by reducing our spending. Immediately. Any nonessentials were immediately cut out of our budget or put on hold. We canceled or froze anything that we didn't deem essential: gym memberships, Amazon monthly deliveries, repeating payments for apps. We were merciless. Once we had an overview of our new budget, we had a clear picture about what we needed to do in order to ensure that we weren't constantly stressed about money or going into our savings to continue living our life. Once we knew what that number looked like, I knew exactly what I needed to bring in until we had a better idea of when the world might open back up. My next step was setting up opportunities to create revenue.

Creating opportunity is the key to living life with a growth mindset, and a crucial step in claiming your confidence. No matter where you are in your life and career journey, the first step toward developing this state of mind is understanding that you should always be looking outside the boundaries that are set for you. Once you realize that the four walls that have been created around an idea, a job, or an opportunity have been created by someone else, you begin to see that there is always another opportunity out there if you have the courage to walk outside the boundaries other people have set for you.

If you are working in a corporate job where your job description is set in stone, this means keeping your eyes open for additional opportunities that will allow you to expand your knowledge. And if your nine-to-five office job doesn't set your world on fire, it means spending time figuring out what fills you up and growing that business alongside your full-time job. And while it is always fun to have a passion project, in this instance as a provider for my family, my next step is always figuring out how to monetize the idea.

The idea for a masterclass series came to me on a run during one of the seemingly endless days of summer early in the pandemic. I am a huge believer in the mind/body connection. There is a part of my mind I can only access while I am running, that allows me to create strategies, figure out complex issues, or simply fix a problem. As I ran, I started thinking about a DM from another person over LinkedIn asking about private coaching in sales. Private coaching had been an impossibility in my life pre-Covid because of my non-stop schedule, and even at the beginning of Covid, the back-to-back Zoom calls made eating lunch a Herculean effort. Since my new role only required me to be in the office three days a week, I now suddenly had more time for coaching. And just like that, the pieces of the puzzle started to fall into place: where there are questions, there is need, and where there is need, there is a market.

When I got home, I DMed the person right back telling them I would be interested in coaching them. Within a few weeks I already had a number of new clients. But after only a few more weeks I realized there was an issue with private coaching: scaling the business. There are only so many hours in the day to do one-on-one sessions. There was clearly a demand for my services, so I needed to think bigger. To work smarter and more efficiently. If my goal was to make money, I needed to scale my business. In order to do that, I needed to reach more people in less time. I had noticed the uptick in messages and questions about private coaching on four topics: sales, negotiations, public speaking, and networking. By that point I was getting a request almost daily in one of those four areas.

Over the next few days, I spent time researching different ways to launch an online class, caucused my friends to talk about platforms they had seen and pricing for classes. I had so much positive feedback that I quickly came to realize that I was thinking too small. I needed to apply my growth mindset and market my skills to a larger audience and hold the class for a number of people at the same time. What I really needed was a way to differentiate this class from everything else I was seeing on Instagram. Just like when writing a book, you need to find your angle, to figure out what will make someone send you a DM to join your class instead of doing something similar online.

If you're like me, whenever I feel insecure or out of my comfort zone, my first instinct is to talk myself out of doing whatever is making me feel like that in the first place. If you deal with this issue as well, face it head-on. Talk yourself *into* it anytime you feel yourself running for the hills. Knowing your weaknesses is as important as knowing your strengths because it helps you create a strategy to handle those issues. Whenever I am in a place where I doubt my ability to do something, I write a list of all the obstacles that might keep me from staying the course. In this case, I had two obstacles:

1. I was worried what everyone would think about me charging money in such a public way.
2. I had no idea how to take payment if anyone did sign up.

On the topic of my first point, I gave myself the same talk I would have given a friend in a similar situation: Who cares what people think? You need to make money. Make money and be proud of it.

Second point? The one thing I learned from taking charity auctions is that you need to get credit card information before the auction, so people don't have the opportunity to back out of the sale. Buyer's remorse is a real thing—especially if someone is given a few days to think about it.

I had never sold anything using social media, so I wasn't exactly sure where to start. I did what I always do when I am stuck on a problem in business: I ask for help. I reach out to someone in my network who has mastered that question to ask for advice. If they don't have the solution, I ask if they can refer me to someone else. I am the first one to offer my network or business advice to anyone who asks and have no qualms about asking other people for advice. What is knowledge if we keep it to ourselves?

I have spoken to so many women over the years who express hesitancy when they think about launching a company or a business because they are too embarrassed to ask anyone else for help. Asking for help is not vulnerability, it is power. How many young women don't reach out to their peers to talk about compensation? As I mentioned earlier, how many young moms don't reach out to ask for help because they want to seem like they are Mom of the Year? How many executives sit in a meeting when they don't understand what is going on but are fearful to ask because they feel like it makes them look junior? When you reach out to people in your network who have mastered a skill set that you do not possess, you are activating your network the way that a network is supposed to be used. Your knowledge is infinitely greater simply because you have access to answers that you don't have time to figure out. Think of it as a valuable use of your precious time. Shortcuts are part of the growth mindset. You don't need to spend time figuring out every single thing if you have a network that can help you.

To solve my payment issue, I decided to reach out to a friend who owns a direct-to-consumer fashion company called Buru. Like many entrepreneurs, she has a growth mindset on steroids, constantly evolving her business model to keep up with her creative mind. She founded her company while pregnant with her first child, when she realized there wasn't a website that curated great clothes for women who wanted pieces they could wear after they finish having babies, that could stay in their closet forever. She began by carefully curating a collection of clothes by top designers that were attractive for women in their early years of motherhood: cue elastic waistbands, zippered tops for easy nursing access, and a lot of fun accessories to take you from the playground to a dinner date. As she progressed through three pregnancies of her own, she eventually realized that she was intimately aware of what moms wanted in all stages of their pregnancy journey and beyond. So she began designing her own. Within a few years she had completely phased out other designers in lieu of her own pieces. Her fabulous, well-priced designs took off and her business skyrocketed. I have so much admiration for her and am awed by her growth mindset. She is also one of the hardest working women I know—she and her husband now run the whole company: they are the business owners, photographers, models, social media team, and the list goes on. I knew that if anyone could answer my question about selling on Instagram, it would be her.

As I was planning to launch the masterclass, I texted to ask for a few minutes of her time to talk through strategies for payments on social media. Ten minutes later we were on the phone. You want something done? Give it to two moms with three kids each. After a minute of catching up, she immediately launched into business mode, giving me a crash course on different payment options. Suddenly a process that seemed daunting felt easy. Her best advice: "Sometimes if I don't know how to do something, I set the timer for a countdown on Instagram before a sale and it forces me to figure it out." She was referring to the timer device on Instagram, a device to promote time-sensitive events and offers and keep your audience informed. Nothing like a deadline! I decided to follow the same advice and set a date and time that would force me to figure it out and make it happen.

The final and most important decision was figuring out the sales pitch for the class. When you are growing a business, you need to have a rock-solid pitch that helps entice a large audience in a short amount of time. There was so much white noise on Instagram, so many people selling their services with a cute post and a fun caption. But in my opinion, a class on sales needed an in-person sales pitch. My pitch needed to appeal to the person who was stuck physically in lockdown but also mentally. It needed to spark a fire in the person who was bored, anxious, and scared of what was happening around them; it needed to galvanize those who felt stuck.

I set a countdown timer clock for a Sunday afternoon on IG Live in order to force myself to do it. I spent the next few days trying out my sales pitch on everyone—my sister, sister-in-law, mom, and friends—to get different perspectives on what they liked about the pitch or felt it was lacking. While we may have one angle on a pitch, it's always important to understand how your sales pitch will be received. Trying it out on others also helps you fine-tune it to include different audiences and perspectives. If everyone had been lukewarm about the pitch, I would have continued to revise it until they felt like it was something they would purchase. You only get one shot to make a first impression, and I needed to make this count.

The concept was simple: I was selling ninety-minute master-classes in four different categories: sales, negotiations, public speaking, and networking. The hook was similar to a sample-sale or a flash-sale model: a short timeline for sign-up, with limited supply; only twenty-five seats available. I wanted people at home to be as frantic that they were going to miss out on a seat in the class as they would have been if Manolo Blahnik were selling shoes for $9.99 to the first hundred customers. Cue Black Friday–crazed shoppers crashing my Instagram. Every Sunday in the month of August I would reveal one of the four masterclass topics for a class that would take place on Thursday afternoon of the same week. Since I was not supposed to be in the office two days a week, I decided to use the afternoon on one of those days to hold the class. Twenty-five seats were available to the first twenty-five people who DMed me and paid the invoice for two hundred dollars. I could coach twenty-five people at the same time instead of spending twenty-five hours coaching everyone who had sent messages. There was also the benefit of a new network of twenty-five people who could support each other far beyond the Zoom class. I began thinking of it like *The Most Powerful Woman in the Room Is You* in class form.

On a sweltering afternoon in August 2020, I stared into the camera of my iPhone watching the clock as it moved closer and closer to 3:00 p.m. As I watched the minutes pass, I tried to remember my talking points for my upcoming LIVE on Instagram. I was nervous: desperately trying to smooth the frizz out of my hair, applying and reapplying lipstick, shifting in my seat, and praying my kids wouldn't run in to request a snack. Truth be told, I wasn't nervous about going live on IG. I'd already spent the first two months of Covid hosting a daily Instagram Live. I'd become comfortable speaking into the small camera on the top of my phone, giving people at home a little hope by highlighting women who were facing the same challenges that we were all facing during the pandemic. We were homeschooling kids, remote working, running businesses, and dealing with our worlds turned upside down while trying to keep everything moving forward.

I was nervous because instead of volunteering my expertise, as I have done much of my adult life, I was charging for it. Time is money and I was ready to make that phrase a reality in my own life. It felt different because it *was* different. While nervous energy is something that I have come to expect to bring an added dose of adrenaline to any speaking opportunities, now the additional element of needing to make money quickly was the motivator I needed to pitch with persuasion.

I had heard Sallie Krawcheck, the founder of Ellevest, an online financial investing platform for women, speak at an event right before the pandemic. During her speech she made a comment about the difference between men's relationship with money versus women's relationship with money. "Women," she said, "think of money as something that should be saved and put under a mattress. Men think of money as a river that ebbs and flows." It was time to make my side business turn into a rushing river.

At 2:59 p.m. I could feel a tingling energy in my fingers and toes mixing with the telltale sign that I am out of my comfort zone: fear. It was time to stop talking. It was time to move forward and make something happen.

At 3:00 p.m. I took a deep breath, hit the LIVE button on the bottom of my phone, smiled directly into the camera, and started my pitch.

"I know everyone is ready for this year to end. We are all tired of this year, tired of spending our days reacting to the bad news, the negativity, always on the back foot. Everyone wants to put 2020 in the rearview mirror. *I* see blue sky and opportunity. It's time to turn this year around. August is over halfway through the year, so let's stop looking backward and thinking about this past. Make this the year you learn to take control of the future."

I always know when something I am saying to an audience or a crowd will touch people because I can feel it. I get goose bumps, tears spring to my eyes, and my voice gets caught in my throat. I knew that the sales pitch would work because I felt like I was talking to myself as much as I was talking to the people jumping on the IG Live. I also knew I needed to hear it as much as anyone watching did. "Be ready with a new skill set so you can hit the ground running when the world opens up again. Twenty-five seats, two hundred dollars a seat."

The first masterclass sold out in two hours. Over the course of the next three weeks, the next three classes sold out as well. Just like that, I had created a revenue stream monetizing my greatest skill, experience.

A couple of days before my first masterclass, *How to Nail a Sale*, I sent a message to all the participants asking a few questions about why they were taking the class. As I read the responses the day of the class, I noticed an interesting thing. Twenty-three out of twenty-five people mentioned confidence. They talked about their lack of confidence and their overwhelming sense of uncertainty during a global pandemic. They wrote about fearing that they were perceived as lacking in confidence, which in turn made them lose any confidence they might have felt. Once I read it on the questionnaires, I realized that I had also heard it everywhere. Confidence had evaporated for so many people in the years following the pandemic. Jobs lost, pay cuts taken, industries upended overnight. The solid foundation that so many people believed would forever remain disappeared. Over the next three weeks I taught the next three masterclasses with twenty-five people each. At the end of the month I reread all the answers and realized that ninety-one out of the one hundred questionnaires mentioned the word "confidence."

And just like with the masterclass, I saw a white space. My next book would be about confidence, because people wanted to know how to find it, or find it again. Where there is a white space there is a business opportunity. But you don't see any of these opportunities unless you approach life with a growth mindset. Your business, and your life, will not grow unless you allow your mind to be open to each and every opportunity. The answer is always YES. Even if you don't know how to do something, you can figure it out.

Growth comes with time and experience, but you can start working on your growth mindset at any time by simply seeking out challenges that force you out of your comfort zone. It is easy to settle into a routine that is comfortable and safe, a routine that doesn't push you and allows for a steady pace. If you are in a job where you feel comfortable and complacent, there might be the temptation to stay there forever. Why rock the boat, right? There are certainly times in life when that is necessary for your well-being. But there will also be a time when you are ready to break out of that comfortable place and try something new. I like to think of growth mindset as a sprint. Before the sprint you need to rest, to sit back and assess the landscape until the white space begins to appear. Once you see it you push hard to make it happen, bringing anyone who can see the vision along with you. With a growth mindset you are always looking out for the next opportunity, as well as seeking them out constantly. Complacency cannot exist when it comes to developing and growing your next great idea. During the pandemic, I watched a close friend start working as a Rodan + Fields rep, selling beauty products to her friends online. On Instagram she did exactly what you see so many beauty influencers do—wash their face with different cleansers and talk about how this business changed their life. She called one day to talk about her frustration with what she was trying to build. I was honest with her.

"You need to build your community by talking to them about what you know, what sets you apart," I told her. "People want to know who you are and what you stand for before they start trusting you to buy your products." Over the next few months, her angle changed. She started to talk candidly about being a stay-at-home mom of three kids trying to transition from being a full-time mom to being an entrepreneur. Within a few months she had dropped the Rodan + Fields business and transitioned to online workshops for moms who needed the encouragement that she had never been able to find. She also started a podcast called *Momplex*, encouraging other stay-at-home moms looking to add "entrepreneur" to their résumé. To me, this is a perfect example of a growth mindset: following the thread and launching something into a white space that you can see.

Following that thread became crucial for me after the masterclass in order to keep evolving. My original concept for the masterclass was a four-week session with one class a week. When the first session was sold out and I had a short waiting list, I decided to hold the entire masterclass series again two months later. I continued holding the entire masterclass series throughout the next year. I also added additional classes when I realized that I was receiving the same questions over and over again.

Soon there were also other revenue-generating opportunities that had never occurred to me. Part of a growth mindset is being open to each and every opportunity. When someone missed the masterclass they asked if I would send them a recording and do a half hour session with them instead. The answer was, of course, yes. Would I do my masterclass for the sales team at a direct-to-consumer company for thirty thousand people? Would I join one of the top jewelry companies in the world on a two-day retreat to give them all four sessions of the masterclass? Yes, I will. Yes, I will indeed. Would I barter my masterclass for a couple of pieces from one of the top fashion houses in the world? No-brainer.

The biggest secret about having a growth mindset is that the answer is always yes. If you don't know how to do something, chances are you can figure it out. Building a business or a side hustle means that there will be many days when you will feel completely out of your comfort zone. Get used to that feeling because the bigger your goals, the more uncomfortable you will be as you figure out how to achieve them.

Opportunity is always out there if you are willing to try something outside of your comfort zone. Look around you, think about what you have that you can teach other people, and think about how you can grow that opportunity. When you look at life with a growth mindset, you have no choice but to own your confidence, secure in the belief that no one else will create a path for you. It depends on what you see in front of you, and how you live your life according to that plan.

A growth mindset will ensure that no matter the twists and turns that life takes you on—and there will be many, trust me—you have enough confidence to believe that you can see through all the chaos and find a way to grow in life and in business. Finally, remember that if you are growing a business, it is important to bring people along for the ride. People like to be part of the journey, to be there at the start when things are gritty and tough, not only when success arrives in all its glory. Sometimes the answers will show themselves in time and have very little to do with what you originally thought your business might look like in the end. Whatever it is, by always showing up with a growth mindset, you will be ready to take it to the next level. Start today, move before you are ready, and who knows, your next idea could be the one that gives you the life you have always wanted.

STEPHANIE SUMMERSON HALL

Founder of Estelle Colored Glass

I grew up with a mom who never stopped; she would not allow you to be lazy if you tried. She was always baking, decorating, and overall a true entrepreneur, full of energy, which she credits with becoming a vegetarian. She modeled hard work and always going after what you want. I channeled these lessons by aiming high with my academics and setting career goals, including a goal to attend law school. After attending law school and practicing for ten years, I had no fear in leaving this field and moving on to entrepreneurship. Ironically, my mom did not understand at all given the perceived prestige of the law field and how hard I had worked to get there. After I made up my mind to move on from law because I had more of a passion for business, I immersed myself fully and learned all I could from other creatives, but I brought my lawyering skill set and natural business acumen to everything I did. I started small and got one solid business venture going, which led to new smaller ventures, with some failing along the way. The failures culminated in my most successful business venture to date, and came to life because I refused to sit on the sidelines. Instead I set goals, and put every ounce of my being into achieving them. Every move forward, and even the setbacks, pushed me closer to reaching my goals. I am proactive in every area of my life because I believe the Bible verse that says, "faith without works is dead." Each time I reach a goal, I set a new goal.

10

POWER YOUR POSITIVITY

A lot of people think the world is divided into two types of people: those who see the glass as half-empty and those who see the glass as half-full. According to this theory, the person who sees the glass as half-full lives in a world of sunshine and rainbows. Nothing seems to bother them. On the flip side, a person who is a glass-half-empty type is trailed by a dark rain cloud wherever they go. The reality is that neither of these perceptions are true. There is no glass, empty or full. Your life is what you make of it, and no matter what your natural disposition, it is possible to *create* positivity every single day, to shift your thinking and your attitude to look for the positive in every situation.

I believe that positivity is a conscious choice, not a personality trait. It is just as easy to be negative as it is to be positive in every aspect of your life. There is no question that some people are born with a twinkle in their eye, just as others seem to have come into this world without that trait. However, even if you don't walk around feeling like you have a pocketful of sunshine, you can still train your mind to act and think in a positive way. It's well worth the effort: to own your confidence is to excel in the language of positivity and share that message with those around you.

The reality is most of us have a temperament that falls somewhere in the middle of the positivity spectrum. We have good days, we have bad days, and we have a few days that are complete outliers on both sides. If you want to be the person who "always looks on the bright side" you are going to have to work to build that muscle to be strong and agile in the face of things that make you want to curl up in a ball and retreat from the world. To get there, you need to begin to own the way you act, analyze what went wrong when you find yourself in a negative headspace, and be conscious of the words you use with other people. It certainly isn't always easy to be positive, but by practicing when the stakes are low, you will ensure that when you are faced with something more challenging, you will have what it takes to find that sliver of happiness even in the darkest of times.

A light snow was falling one December morning when I slipped quietly into the kitchen of our apartment. I was always a night owl until I had children, but now I love waking up early in the morning to sit quietly with a cup of coffee and get ready for the day. I find looking out a window as the snow falls down on the streets of New York particularly magical because snow didn't play a big part in my childhood.

When I was growing up in Louisiana, winter wasn't something that was discussed because the temperatures rarely dipped below fifty degrees. Snow was such a rarity that even a small flurry meant school was canceled and people were scared to drive because, you know, Southerners don't know how to drive in the snow. As a result, I have spent my entire life praying for warmth, despite the fact that I have lived in New York for twenty years. All to say, my southern upbringing is my first line of defense when explaining my lack of preparedness for anything snow-related, which, as you will see, can be a real problem.

As usual, my quiet morning ended abruptly as my kids came tumbling out of bed in various stages of awake around seven. Within minutes we were in full "breakfast, get ready for school, did you really brush your teeth, put on your shoes so we can walk out of the house" mode. I had an early meeting, so I was taking our two oldest kids to school while my husband had a later start because he was taking our little one to school.

As typically happens on days when things completely fall apart, it all started off so well. The kids were dressed and ready to walk out on time. We weren't in a rush, and, as usual, my youngest daughter used the opportunity to get as many hugs and kisses as humanly possible from her siblings before I ushered them into the elevator to take us down to the street.

In the mornings as we walk out onto the busy street my pulse always skips a beat. It's like a switch flips and life becomes super-charged with people striding purposefully down the sidewalk, taxis honking, and the noises of a city waking up. Raising three kids in New York is an adventure in so many ways. At least once a week I remind them how lucky we are to be able to live in a city where we walk out the door and there is immediately something to see or something to do. Not to mention that we are never dependent on a car—we can just put on a pair of shoes and walk anywhere we want to go.

As we walked down the street that morning, the kids chattered excitedly about the upcoming holiday events at school. I half listened while mentally reviewing talking points for a huge presentation that morning. I wanted to be ready to go the minute I walked in the door; that meant practicing even when I wasn't on my own. I want to be present for my kids as much as possible, but I also understand that not every moment in life is a present moment when you are juggling life as a busy mom with a nonstop job. Let the guilt go.

As we neared the subway entrance, a light snow was falling and my kids squealed with delight as they tried to catch snowflakes on their tongues. New York with a light dusting of snow is so picture perfect that we made it all the way down the subway steps before realizing that the kids didn't have their backpacks for school. Since we were already walking into the subway, I contemplated forgetting the backpacks altogether—but homework was due, so we hurried back home, grabbed the backpacks, gave an extra hug/kiss combo to a happily surprised Eloise, and then headed back into the elevator and down to the street.

In the ten minutes it took to pick up the backpacks and walk back to the subway, the sky began to exhibit signs of my least favorite winter weather, which the meteorologists refer to as "wintry mix." Now I was bemoaning the fact that I hadn't grabbed an umbrella when we stopped at the apartment.

All was not lost as we heard the subway pulling in as we descended into the station. We quickly walked down the stairs and hopped right on. I glanced at my phone; it was a little later than I hoped, but we still had plenty of time. Four stops later we hopped off the subway and walked up the steps. I groaned as I saw that the snow/sleet had turned into sleet/heavy rain while we were underground. I pulled my coat over my head, encouraged the kids to do the same, and we half walked/half jogged the three blocks to school.

By the time I opened the door to leave their school, the sleet had become a heavy downpour of rain. I considered getting an Uber, but during rush hour I would add half an hour to my commute and the surge pricing meant my ride to Midtown was equivalent to a plane ticket to California. My best option was to run to the subway three blocks away, which would deliver me underneath my building at work. I glanced at my phone again—I was cutting it VERY CLOSE. *Okay, Lydia—new plan—get to the office, pull wet hair into a bun, and throw on some lipstick. Buns are chic, right?*

I ran through the rain, my hair sticking to my face as I prayed that a train would be pulling in just as I arrived. I practically jumped down the subway steps to the subway entrance, swiped my Metro-Card, and dashed through the subway turnstile. As I ran through the Union Square subway tunnel toward the stairs leading to the subway, I saw that my train was arriving in two minutes.

Finally, a stroke of luck.

Or so I thought.

Then I made the mistake that completely changed my day. My sliding doors moment, if you will. I started to run. Since hindsight is 20/20, I can say with complete certainty that if I had done the opposite, if I had slowed down, knowing that I would reach the train in time, my day would have been completely different. But I didn't. I'm a runner, and if I think I can get somewhere faster, I run for it.

Remember what I said earlier about snow? Well, one other thing I didn't consider in the two seconds it took for me to start running was that some of the wet snow/sleet/rain had formed a very slick layer on the subway floor which meant when I sped up, I slipped. I don't mean slipped and caught myself or that I fell neatly on the ground. I mean slipped as in arms flailing, legs flying out in every direction as I desperately tried not to fall and instead ended up falling forward, sliding on my hands and knees while my tote bag emptied upside down on the messy, snowy, dirty subway floor in front of me.

I stayed on my hands and knees for a second, stunned by what had happened, performing a quick mental check to make sure nothing felt broken. When I was certain that nothing was bruised except for my ego, I reached out to start retrieving my belongings that were scattered around me. In true New York fashion, no one stopped to help. People walked right by as if I wasn't crawling around scooping up my wallet, keys, and phone on a dirty subway platform. I stood up and glanced down, noticing that my tights were ripped on the knee but otherwise I seemed to be okay. It was at that moment that I realized I might still be able to make the train. I cautiously walked down the stairs, gripping the railing like I was on a roller-coaster ride holding on for dear life, and stepped onto the subway platform just as the subway doors were closing, arriving defeated by the turn of events.

As the doors closed in front of me, I caught a glimpse of my reflection in the window of the subway door. I saw myself the way that anyone around me would see me at that moment: outstretched hands covered in dirt, soaking wet hair, and my face filled with frustration. It was as if the world had conspired against me to destroy my best-laid plans and there was nothing I could do about it. It was 8:45 in the morning, and the day was already ruined. I was late for my meeting, covered in mud, with ripped tights, a dirty purse, and soaking wet hair. It was so easy to be angry at the day, angry at the circumstances, angry at myself for running despite the fact that there are signs everywhere on the subway platforms that warn DO NOT RUN.

In that moment, as I stared at myself in the reflection as the train started to pull away, I recognized how much power my frustration and rage had over everyone around me. Such power that could be used in all the wrong ways. I could use my anger to ruin the day of everyone around me starting this very minute. This wretched mood could be like a pebble tossed into a pond, causing ripples in every direction. I had the power to wreck the day of everyone who crossed my path from that moment on. Carrie Bradshaw said it best in *Sex and the City*: "New York is a great place to be in love, but it's an even better city to be angry."

I could wait for the next subway to arrive and shove my way past the people disembarking instead of stepping back to allow them to get off, as I have seen so many people do. After leaving the subway, I could walk into Starbucks and stand frustrated, glaring at the baristas as they made my coffee in as short a time as humanly possible. I could direct my poisonous mood at the person behind the counter checking me out from lunch, the person who accidentally bumped me as I walked down the street, every member of my team by using my irritated mood on them over a small mistake. I could let my mood impact my kids from the moment I picked them up after school, or my husband when he arrived home from work, and on and on and on. Anger is such an easy emotion with immediate results. You can watch the physical reaction of someone else as you direct your anger toward them, watch their eyes narrow as they react to the negativity you direct at them, at the negativity that you have inserted into their day. That would make me feel better, right?

As I watched the rear lights of the subway car disappear into the tunnel, I was left alone on the platform. As the minutes ticked by, I could feel the initial burn of anger start to dissipate and I thought about one of my favorite expressions, "If you have one argument in a day it's 50/50, if you have more than one you should look in a mirror." As I thought about that expression it made me think about myself. What if it didn't only apply to other people in your life? What if that applied to your own mindset as well? What if in the moments where we are at our darkest, angriest, lowest of the low we challenge ourselves to do the opposite? To think outside ourselves, about how our actions in that moment could impact those around us. To look for the good and then to act as the good, the positive, to inspire positivity. Not just in ourselves, but in those around us. To realize that the world is not centered around us, but rather we are one of many, and our actions can impact as many others with negativity as they can with a positive outlook.

I wondered: *What if I spent the next few minutes waiting for the train reframing the narrative of my morning?* Reframing and retelling the story of what happened not as a series of negative, unrelated instances that occurred, but rather looking for the positive moments instead. That morning, on the dirty, disgusting subway platform, standing with ripped tights and God-only-knows-what on my hands, I waited for the train and did just that. I focused on the extra kiss and hug from my surprised little Eloise when we forgot Henry's backpack, the first walk to the subway where Beatrice and Henry were trying to catch snowflakes on their tongues, the fact that my legs were healthy and strong enough to run for the train—even if that hadn't yielded the desired results, and that I had a job I loved.

I reframed my day in gratitude and positivity for the things that I had that allowed me to run for that train and I thought about how I could use this story to make everyone laugh. To make them feel better about their morning instead of ruining the day of everyone around me. During this moment of quiet introspection, I realized that this story could be my day zero of turning my life around and truly harnessing the power of positive thinking. I have had a positive outlook in my life, but never, until that day, did I think about what I could do to change the entire course of my day—and the day of everyone around me.

We harness our power when we are confident enough to understand that we have control over every aspect of ourselves. Not the situations around us or the things that happen to us, but our reaction to the hard times, the difficult moments, the things that seem unfair.

The next time you find yourself in a situation where things seem to be piling on, use the opportunity to pause and claim your confidence. Stop dwelling in the negative and actively seek out the positive in whatever has occurred. Stop thinking about yourself. Stop thinking about you as the center of your universe of one. Look outward instead of inward. Focus your energy on others, not on yourself. The way in which you approach problems, issues, situations with a positive mindset isn't just for you. Will it help you succeed, will it bring people to you because of your positive attitude, will you feel better because of it? Yes. But the power of positivity doesn't just change the day for you, it changes the day for everyone around you.

In the same way that negativity is powerful, positivity is infectious. So empower yourself to spread that positivity around starting today. Wherever you are, whatever you are doing, I want you to give power to positivity in your life. Over the next week, find three moments where you feel a negative emotion—someone said something unkind, you didn't get something you wanted, or even something simpler, that your coffee is taking a long time to make in a busy coffee shop. Embrace it, let it ruminate—annoyance, anger, irritation—really feel it. And then pause, take a deep breath, and think about what you can do to change that emotion and power your positivity.

The only person who has to know you are making this internal shift is you. If you can't power your positivity every single time, don't worry. You will have plenty of chances to practice all day, every day. So start small. The next time you are in a long line that feels like water torture, when you feel your blood pressure starting to rise, do the following: wait until you reach the person who is checking everyone out and then look them straight in the eye, flash them a big smile, and say thank you like you mean it, with flourish! "THANK YOU!," you will exclaim with a huge smile. "I HOPE YOU ARE HAVING A GREAT DAY!" Try it with someone who is making your morning cup of coffee, your waiter at a restaurant, or someone who is getting eye rolls from everyone as they try to do their job. Think about how many people stare at their phones without engaging with the world around them or look up quickly only to show annoyance at the extra minute it takes for someone to do their job. Then watch how looking someone straight in the eyes and thanking them with a confident smile is mirrored back to you. How it reflects in the way that they engage and interact with the next person they greet or engage with in a day. By giving yourself the power to understand that your actions can affect everyone around you, you start to understand the most important thing about confidence. Confidence comes with ownership, from owning your words, your actions, and their impact on others. From knowing that every action you make has a ripple effect on your day and the day of everyone around you. It all starts with you, and that all starts within.

A few minutes later the train arrived, and I stepped back to allow everyone to get off before I even took my first step onto the train. I put my earbuds in and pumped up an upbeat, positive song and willed myself to stay in this positive zone.

And you know what? It worked.

By the time I arrived in the office the meeting was well underway. I had a few texts from the team asking where I was as the meeting began and I texted back: Subway delay start without me, I'll be there as soon as possible. I quickly ran into the restroom, thoroughly scoured my hands with soap in an effort to remove whatever man-eating bacteria I had surely picked up from the platform of a NYC subway, pulled my hair back in a bun, then took off the tights and threw them in the trash. I walked calmly into the meeting with a big smile on my face, laughingly told them that the subway delay was my fault because of a catastrophic fall on the subway platform, and apologized for being late.

As my colleague continued with her portion of the presentation, I listened, engaged by what she was saying, and asked a quick question at the end. As she finished up the final Q & A, we were nearly out of time. I asked the team if they could spare five more minutes for the woman whose ego had taken a major bashing earlier in the day. I offered a meeting later in the day to anyone who had to leave, when I could pop by and explain the presentation one-on-one. I kept my tone positive and light. There was no anger, no frustration passed along to anyone around me. I was not going to make the fact that I chose to run on a slippery subway platform the reason that everyone had a bad day.

The presentation went well, no one lived or died as a result of my being late, and, more important, that moment about positive mindset stayed with me long past that day.

Since that morning on the subway, I have repeated that phrase back to myself many times when I find my reactions are out of sorts. On the days when traffic is horrible, work emails endless, the kids seem to have turned on each other in a moment that seems oddly reminiscent of a scene from *The Hunger Games*, or I've stepped into a puddle and ruined my favorite pair of shoes, the world is not conspiring against me. Each of these situations on its own is irritating and frustrating, but just because these things are all happening within an hour does not mean that the rest of your day can't be good. You always have the power to change the course of the day and, more importantly, your reaction to situations both positive and negative.

You might be thinking, "That might work sometimes, but how do you do that when you wake up on the wrong side of the bed or feel like the world isn't turning in your favor?" If you want to have a positive mindset, you need to start your day off with a positive mindset. The next time you wake up and feel that negative energy spiraling within you, physically stop what you are doing and take a couple of minutes to say out loud one thing you are grateful for in your life. Even if you are going through an incredibly difficult time, remember that everyone faces difficult moments in life. You are not alone in having a difficult moment, you are one of many who probably woke up having a bad day. But here is the difference. You know that you aren't going to let it ruin your day. You aren't going to let it ruin the day of others. You are going to take ownership of your life and believe that you and you alone control the narrative of your day. If you are in such a low moment that you can't find the happiness, seek an external hype moment—for me that means turning up the volume on a top 40 song and singing loudly with my kids while we are getting dressed, having that extra cup of coffee even though I know it might make me a little jittery for part of the day, calling a friend who makes me laugh to get me out of a negative headspace. Whatever you do, don't start your day in the negative because it all starts there. If you leave your house and within an hour find yourself crawling across a subway platform on your hands and knees, allow yourself to find humor in the situation. Make light of it. You don't think you are in control of the positivity in your life, but you are. We all are. Don't let yourself hide in the shadows of negativity. Step into the spotlight of your life and enjoy the shine that positivity brings to you and everyone around you.

Confidence comes with ownership. Ownership of a moment, a situation that presents itself to you and your reaction to it. If you are constantly allowing other people to dictate your mood or giving energy to things that don't go your way, you are taking power away from yourself and giving it to anyone or anything that crosses your path. If you commit to holding on to that power, you begin to understand that you are the architect of everything that happens to you because you control your response to it—both positive and negative. A confident person walks into a room understanding that no matter what happens, they can handle it. It might not be what they expect or want to happen, but they can work with it and continue to shape their own narrative.

While committing to this in your daily life is incredibly important, I also find that it is imperative at work—whether that be in an office, a volunteer position, or as the leader of your home. Life is too short to go to a place you dread every day. Office and home cultures are reflective of the person who leads the team or leads the family. A positive mindset starts at the top, so remember that if you are the leader of a team or a family, never underestimate how much better it is for everyone when you create a positive environment for those around you. If you are leading a team, you set the tone every day when you walk in the door. If you woke up on the wrong side of the bed or, say, slid down an icy, muddy subway platform, do not bring that with you. The minute you walk in with your bad mood, expect everyone around you to meet that mood. Even if every single person walked into the office that morning in a good mood, if the boss walks in fuming and frustrated, expect the entire team to adopt that working style within the hour. It's the trickle-down effect. If you want a happy, positive environment, create it for everyone around you and they will pass it along to everyone they work with—internal and external colleagues alike. The way you treat people who report to you is the way that they will treat people they interact with on your behalf. Your team reflects you, so ensure that the way they treat other people is the way that you would want them to be treated as well.

This also goes for the people who work on your team. If there is one person who is constantly dragging everyone down with their bad attitude, have a frank conversation with them. All it takes is one person to walk in with a negative, combative attitude to put everyone into a bad mood. Effective managers understand that they are responsible for their team in its entirety, so do not allow bad attitudes to drag down your team or your work product. When you are a manager, it is incumbent on you to get in front of it to keep everyone from getting swept up in a wave of negativity.

During the global pandemic, we went from in-person meetings to a completely virtual world overnight. Everyone was reeling from the fear of the unknown, but there was a marked difference in the way that people handled it. Certainly, it was an unprecedented time that we all hope never to repeat, but I was struck by how some people were able to keep moving forward and keep their positive energy up, while others simply could not. For every positive person I spoke with who was looking for the small wins to keep them going throughout the darkest times, there were plenty of others who were more than content to sit in the dark place and bring everyone into that place with them.

This was particularly pronounced on Zoom meetings, which were every half hour all day every day. There was a distinct difference between the meetings where a leader recognized that positivity was critical to maintaining a good work environment and those where they did not. I remember a few calls where I swear the clock was moving backward because the person in charge of the meeting brought the lowest amount of energy possible to the call, and that low energy was matched by everyone else on the call. Even on days when I was feeling less than great, I still felt the responsibility to lead my team by showing them positivity and encouragement whenever possible.

If you are someone who is just starting out in your career, remember that few things will get you as far in an office as a positive attitude and a work ethic to match. Over the years I have worked with some amazing interns, temps, and junior team members who brightened the day from the minute I walked in the door. Those were always the people I gravitated toward from the minute I met them, the ones whom I would ask to walk downstairs when I went to get lunch or a cup of coffee. I am far more likely to engage with people who walk in with a positive attitude looking to be helpful, rather than someone who walks in the office wearing earbuds and walks out later in the day with the earbuds still firmly in place. When you are starting out in your career, be the person who brings positivity to the office and gifts it to everyone around you. If you are having the worst day of your life, you might want to skip that strategy for the day, but don't use the office as a dumping ground for negativity. Your office life is just beginning. Set the tone from day one and realize that being someone who brings a positive attitude to work will always be rewarded for it.

Of course, no matter how hard you try to keep a positive mindset, there are unforeseen events that shake even the most positive among us to the core. The global pandemic was something that none of us could have imagined in our wildest dreams, and no matter how positive I kept my mindset, there were many moments when I could barely hold on to the lesson that I had learned about the importance of a positive mindset that day on the subway. It was a time when all of us had to push ourselves to find even the smallest thread of positivity to keep going.

Living in New York City in the winter of 2021 was not for the faint of heart. If there was one word that does not come to mind during that time it was positivity. Gone was the bustling city I have lived in for two decades, teeming with people striding purposefully to live up to their full potential. Every morning when I walked out of my apartment, I had to recalibrate my thinking. *It must be a Sunday*, I would think, since Sunday is always a quiet day in the city. No, it's Monday at 8:30 a.m., the neighborhood should be packed, the coffee shops with lines out the door. Instead, it was an eerily empty city.

Any places we might have taken our children were closed, and no one wanted to host any type of indoor playdate lest they become the super-spreader that would infect someone with Covid. Social media was on fire, decrying the death of New York City as a place no one wanted to live anymore since it was ground zero for the global pandemic. To many, if you could figure out a way to make it happen, a much smarter strategy was to leave for good. Why would you stay in a place where Covid was raging and every facet of life required you to be in a small space with complete strangers?

Don't get me wrong. I saw what they saw. I saw the piles of trash that grew higher every day, the snow piles that filled with trash up and down the streets, the boarded-up stores, the empty storefronts, the broken windows, and graffiti. I saw it, but I refused to pile on with negativity. Instead of constantly listening to the negative comments and nonstop negativity that came from people who had left the city, and the media in general, I trained my mind to constantly recalibrate whatever was in front of me and reframe it in a positive light. I remember walking by an overturned garbage can on the street in Soho with the contents strewn all over the snowy, dirty sidewalk. I stood for a second looking, and said out loud to myself on that deserted street, "Look up, not down." It was a mantra I would repeat to myself daily over the course of the winter. *Look up, not down.* Was there trash on the street? Yes, but trash can be cleaned up. The majesty of the city was still there, even if you had to look a little closer to see it. Whenever I was feeling low, I would look up instead of down. In the early hours after school drop-off, I would walk home to join my first Zoom call watching the sunlight creep up through the narrow cracks in the buildings until it suddenly appeared, bathing the city in light. At night, I would look out of my window watching the lights turn on in the skyscrapers around our apartment, illuminating the cityscape and making me forget we were in the middle of a global pandemic.

New York has been around for hundreds of years, and a couple of tough years would not alter the course of the city in perpetuity. While others saw a ghost city, I would remind myself how incredible it was to walk through this magnificent city alone, to get on a Citi Bike and cycle slowly through neighborhoods without worrying about getting hit by the traffic, or dodging pedestrians so glued to their iPhone they didn't look up as they walked across the street. My husband and I took the kids on long walks through parts of New York City that two years prior had been so busy you could barely move.

I messaged positivity in conversations, on social media, to anyone and everyone who asked about the state of the city. In some ways I forced positivity, knowing that if I allowed that negativity in, it might stay for good. That isn't to say there weren't moments that felt so low and dark that I had to sit with those emotions too, but I didn't let them set up camp and drag my attitude down indefinitely. It's okay to feel frustrated and angry, sad, or upset. There are also times when the low is too low and seeking help is the only answer. I do not want to understate that or minimize this if you have struggled with mental health or continue to find yourself in a dark place that no amount of positive mindset can help. If that is the case for you, please seek help and know that there is power in asking for help. But many of us have the capacity to control our mindset, positive or negative. Emotion is emotion, and you need to feel all of it. Life isn't perfect or easy. It is imperfect and difficult and at times incredibly messy, but learning to power your positivity will show you that you are strong enough to push through those times and see the good. Stay with that feeling and believe in yourself enough to know that you will make it through every single hard, difficult time and thrive.

Throughout your life, there will be plenty of moments when things do not work out the way you hoped, or something happens that feels completely out of your control. Confidence comes from owning your outlook and your reaction to the world around you. Having a positive mindset doesn't mean that everything in your life will always go well, it means that even when things are not going well, when it feels like everything in your life is against you, you can still find the positive in it. And YOU will be okay. Be true to that. Understand how important it is to embrace and nurture that mindset. The next time you find yourself in a situation where you feel like the world is against you, pause, take a deep breath, and think about what you can do to change that perception. And then put the biggest smile on your face and bring your positive message out into the world with confidence. Your life, your story. Make it the story of the life you want to live.

MIGNONNE GAVIGAN SMITH

Founder and COO of Mignonne Gavigan

When I was figuring out what to do with my life after college, my parents encouraged me to follow my dreams. Twenty years later, after a great deal of hard work, I am the founder of Mignonne Gavigan, a jewelry brand specializing in ornately beaded and embroidered pieces made by expert artisans in Mumbai, India. I had a design professor tell me that if I was ever going to start my own line, it needed to be unique, it needed to stand out against all the other lines out there. And I design with those words in mind. The jewelry is meant to be a breath of fresh air, something that makes people happy to wear and happy when they see it. It's my belief that the happiness comes from wearing something that makes you smile, gives you a feeling of confidence, control. There is a reaction to the bright colors, the mix of materials, and the elevated techniques that gives the wearer that unique feeling of joy. And when there's joy, anything is possible.

11

CHANGE IS THE NAME OF THE GAME

*L*adies and gentlemen, please welcome our auctioneer this evening *from Christie's, Lydia Fenet,"* boomed a voice echoing through the cavernous room at Cipriani 42nd Street in Midtown Manhattan. Rotating my gavel in my hand one last time, I strode confidently to the podium looking out at the audience of seven hundred people dressed in brightly colored cocktail dresses and tuxedos staring up at the stage. As I arrived at center stage, my eyes adjusting to the bright lights, I spread my notes across the podium that sat center stage. I picked up the microphone in my left hand and with a huge smile on my face slammed down my gavel, CRACK CRACK CRACK. *It's auction time*, I thought as I picked up the microphone and walked from behind the podium to take command of the stage.

Feeling confident and excited, I launched into my opener: "Good evening, ladies and gentleman, my name is Lydia Fenet and I am so delighted to be here from Christie's . . ." My voice trailed off as

I quickly realized that there was no sound coming from the microphone. I flipped the microphone over to make sure the audiovisual team had switched it on, but a quick look at the bottom revealed that the green light was already on.

I started again, "Good evening, ladies and gentlemen . . ." I paused as I saw a few people shaking their head.

"We can't hear you," said a few voices from the dimly lit ballroom as a low din of people murmuring started to spread across the room. Not exactly off to a stellar start.

I tapped the top of the microphone a few times to hear if there was any sound, but the tapping only confirmed my fear. There was no sound. I looked out at the audience as I tapped it a few more times, keeping a smile on my face. "Is this thing on?"

The crowd continued to shake their heads. I looked stage right to see if the audiovisual team had figured out a solution. One glance at the team gesticulating wildly to each other gave me the answer pretty quickly. I smiled at the audience. "Don't go anywhere, you guys," I joked as I walked over to the edge of the stage.

"Do you have another mike?" I asked, keeping a smile on my face despite the fact that my heart was triple beating. I was almost certain the audience could hear it. From the panicked look on her face I knew the answer.

A general rule in charity auctioneering that will also serve you well in life: when things are not going as planned, remain calm at all costs. If you are the person in charge, people are looking to you for leadership, not to be the one who creates chaos with their panic. I walked to the event planner and handed her the microphone before walking back to the podium. I turned to the audience, most of whom had already lost interest and turned back to their tables to start talking again.

I stood at the podium for a few seconds before deciding. The evening program had already run long, and any further delay might allow people the opportunity to head home early for the night. If we pushed the auction any later, it might take away potential dollars for the nonprofit. This auction needed to start. With or without a microphone.

Take two: I slammed the gavel down to get the attention of the audience. "All right, ladies and gentlemen. Here's the deal. There is no microphone right now." I heard a smattering of laughter from the audience, but continued, "Which, as you can imagine, is probably the worst-case scenario for an auctioneer." I kept a smile on my face the entire time as if I was completely unfazed by this turn of events. "And I have enough faith in this crowd to believe that you would never want to do that to your favorite auctioneer, right?" I heard a few chuckles. "With or without a microphone, I am here to raise money and I need all of you engaged and ready to bid in order to make that happen. You guys in?" The crowd applauded their response. I don't know if they were excited about the prospect of the auction, but they seemed to understand my reasoning. I launched into the first lot as the audience stayed as quiet as a group of seven hundred people possibly could for three minutes. As I slammed the gavel down with a resounding "SOLD!" I saw the event organizer running up onstage to hand me the mike. The audience cheered as the microphone amplified my voice just in time to start the second lot. Never underestimate how much people want you to succeed as a speaker onstage. Everyone loves an underdog, so by sharing your vulnerability, people will get behind you and root for your success.

When I got offstage that night at the auction, one of the new event planners came over to me to get the microphone. She paused for a minute and then said, "You are such a natural, Lydia. You handle change so well—nothing fazes you." I almost laughed out loud. Nothing could be further from the truth, but after almost nineteen years as a charity auctioneer, there is one thing I know: to be truly confident, you need to accept that change is constant. Confidence comes from trusting that you will evolve, change, and keep up with the times no matter what is thrown in front of you.

Throughout my childhood and early adult life, I was always incredibly resistant to change and any type of upheaval. I spent my early twenties fearing change and doing anything I possibly could to mitigate any potential for change or disruption in my life. I fought it, resisted it, and believed that things were only good when they were the same. Whether it was staying in the same place for a job, staying in the same apartment, or even eating the same thing for lunch, I felt safe and comfortable when I knew exactly what was in front of me without any disruption to the plan. But that line of thinking was not doing me any favors. Life is not constant; life is unpredictable. If you can only handle what is in front of you when it's familiar, you aren't preparing yourself for the constantly shifting nature of life. Change will happen, whether or not you are ready for it.

At times, you will need to move before you are ready so you are already moving when the opportunity for change comes. Staying in one place will make you feel as if you are always on the back foot, waiting for things to happen to you. Seek new challenges and opportunities whenever you can and don't be fearful if you don't have everything mapped out. Even if you do have it mapped out, there is a good chance half of your plans will get tossed out the window by something unexpected. Life is filled with uncertainty, so accept it and make it part of your journey.

It isn't until everything is moving along in one direction and the bottom falls out below that you really know how strong you are, and how much you can overcome. Change allows you to not only push yourself out of your comfort zone but grow as a person. By placing you in circumstances you may not have planned for or wanted, change actually helps you. It allows you to adjust your understanding of the parameters of your life and your goals.

There will always be change. Confident, successful people know this, they expect it and anticipate it whenever they can. When they are blindsided in life, they do not bury their head in the sand, but embrace it. The next time the unexpected happens, they draw from their past experience and continue to build on that confidence, to keep moving forward.

As I stood backstage that night listening to the event planner praise me as "a natural," I told her the truth. I knew how to handle that situation not because I am a natural, but because I had been through that scenario multiple times over the course of my career. In fact, over a nineteen-year career as an auctioneer I have been onstage exactly nine times without a working microphone, and I can remember every single time in granular detail. Each time was a little painful, yet each time it happened, it was easier to handle. The sharpness of the embarrassment wore off and I became more and more confident in my ability to take control of the situation. Like anything, getting comfortable with change takes practice, and knowing that you can handle it gives you the ability to handle even more complex and difficult situations in the future.

I will never, ever forget the first time that I took an auction without a working mike because it was the single most humiliating experience in my twenties. It happened during my first year as an auctioneer and I had very little confidence in my auctioneering abilities.

As a newbie auctioneer you are often assigned auctions in New York City for public and private schools. The assumption is that the crowds tend to be kinder because they are usually raising money for their children's school. I showed up as a young, overprepared auctioneer desperate to do a stellar job that would have everyone talking about my performance for weeks on end. Slightly delusional, but you have to be your own greatest cheerleader in life, so don't be afraid to root for yourself. I walked into the gymnasium of a local public school that was decorated in various shades of blue to reflect the Under the Sea theme. I could tell by the crowd at the bar that the parents were on course to set a world record for drinking the most alcohol in the least amount of time. This was, in my opinion, a positive. My hope was that a little extra alcohol might loosen the inhibitions of my bidders later in the evening. As I circled the room trying to find my point of contact, I finally found the event chair for the auction committee, who was dressed, predictably, head to toe in blue.

For the next half hour, we stood by the makeshift stage set up at the end of the gymnasium discussing the lots for the sale. These were not the type of art you would see on the auction block at Christie's, but rather a mixture of children's artwork, class projects, and a vacation home donated by parents of the school. The purpose of the auction was to raise money for the school scholarship fund. As we neared the time set for the auction, I could feel my adrenaline rushing in as we discussed last-minute details.

The chair of the event had mentioned there was video about the school that showed all the kids in their classrooms accompanied by an upbeat soundtrack. Obviously, this was meant to tug at the heart-strings of the parents and coax them into making one more bid. As the designated time for the auction came and went, I watched the well-meaning volunteers desperately try to get parents from the bar area to sit down in the seats near the stage. As it became evident that it was taking a little longer than they originally hoped, an over-served father hopped up onstage and let out a loud wolf whistle to get everyone to the front of the room. Some parents complied, others stayed by the bar, but he was persistent and kept at it until a few more parents drifted up to the front.

Sensing that this approach was futile at best, I leaned over to the event chairs and asked if I could make an announcement that the auction was about to begin. She lit up, "That would be great!"

"Perfect, where is the microphone?" I asked.

She looked at me blankly. "Oh, we don't have a microphone. We thought you would just get up onstage and do your thing."

My thing? I wasn't sure what type of thing I was bringing to the table, but I was fairly confident that "this thing" would not help me engage three hundred loud, overserved people for an hour-and-a-half auction. After ten more minutes of wolf whistles and shushing by the dad, most of the crowd was seated, albeit still chattering noisily. In an effort to draw people to their seats, they decided to bring down the lights and roll the video, hoping that would bring in even the most resistant parents. Luckily, it had the desired effect and as the lights came up, I jumped onto the stage, brought the gavel down, and launched into the auction. And that, my friends, is the only positive thing I can say about the entire night.

Within three minutes it became clear that very few of the guests had any intention of listening to a young auctioneer bumble her way through seventeen lots during their one night out without their kids. There are brutal public speaking experiences, and then there are very brutal public speaking experiences, and then there are experiences that are so humiliating that you almost black out. I'm sure you can guess which category this auction fell in to. I can still remember the burning feeling in my face as people stood up to leave in the first few minutes of the auction to grab a drink. The problem was they never came back, and the bar chatter was so loud that I couldn't even hear my voice over the crowd. Bar: 300, Lydia: 0.

The most ego-crushing moment of that auction was the final lot: a kindergarten class project. By that point there were only three people left in the audience. None of the remaining guests bid on the lot. I hammered down the gavel and ran off the stage and out of the exit door so fast they couldn't have stopped me if they tried. I cried the whole way home and ignored my roommate who was watching TV as she asked, "How was the auction?"

I ran past her and crawled into my bed, my eyes swollen from crying. If that was going to be my new Saturday night, I figured, I could do without it. There had been difficult auctions, without a doubt, but this was a whole new level of bad. It was one of the most embarrassing moments of my auctioneering career. I swore that night I would give up auctioneering entirely.

A few weeks later, I was sitting at my desk when I received an email from a fellow auctioneer. A client was coming into town later that week and he needed to take him out for dinner. He asked if I could take his auction. At first I ignored the email, the sting of embarrassment from the last auction still fresh in my mind. But after sitting on the email for two days, I finally emailed him back and agreed to take it. Later that week, I nervously stood stage right, this time with a working mike. The minute I walked onstage I felt the embarrassment of the last auction fade. In fact, that auction and the subsequent auctions almost erased the memory entirely. Almost.

Two years later, I found myself onstage with a microphone that started dropping sound every few seconds. Although I thought about powering through, it was so distracting I couldn't think of anything else. It was another painful moment, but certainly not as painful as the first experience without the microphone. As I stood backstage waiting for the AV team to fix the mike so I could go back onstage, I realized that this was likely not going to be the last time I had an issue onstage. Instead of dreading it and freezing up, I needed to approach it as an opportunity to rise and meet the challenge. No matter what happened, the show needed to go on.

Each of the unexpected experiences here was teaching me an invaluable lesson. In order to be truly confident, you have to throw out the script of a perfectly orderly life. You have to believe in yourself enough to know that no matter what life throws at you, you are capable. And each time you confront an obstacle, you add to an arsenal that will equip you for bigger challenges and bigger changes along the way. An athlete does not win an Olympic gold their first time in the pool, they spend years building and building on their skills. They adjust, they course correct, they lose, they win. The same can be said for building up your ability to accept change. The more you accept that change is part of your story, the more you will be able to handle it when the unexpected comes your way.

There will never be a situation you can't overcome when you believe that accepting change is part of any process. Learning to embrace change will shape you into the most confident version of yourself. It is equally important to reflect on the lessons each time you go through them, so you can empower yourself to keep moving forward. It's okay to feel fear and be wary of change, but know that when you learn to accept change and roll with the punches, you are building a stronger version of yourself. A version of yourself that you can trust to stay strong even when everything around you is falling apart.

The next time you find yourself in a situation where you feel yourself resisting change, I challenge you to take the opposite approach.

When you are confronted with change, when you feel your body tense up, feel out of control or scared of the unknown, try something that will give you power and put you in control of the situation.

Start by visualizing what you are fearful of in that moment. What is making you feel resistance to change? The possibility of a negative outcome? Scared of the unknown? Maybe both? Take a long, deep breath. Think about the worst-case scenario, the worst outcome from that change, and sit with that emotion until you can articulate exactly what it is that is making you feel this anxiety. Now, the most important part. Reach out to a ride-or-die friend – you know, the one you call in equal measure to ask for an outfit recommendation or after you've had the best date of your life? Tell them all about this change and what scares you about the change. Talking about things that challenge us, that become emotions that sit in our stomach like a stone and make us feel like we can't move, makes them lose power. The more we talk, the less power these things have over our emotions. Once you have taken away the power that might make you stop embracing the change, map out three different ways that this change could go and how you would react, so you feel like you are in control of the situation. By looking ahead without fear, you will not find yourself in a place where you are waiting to react to what is coming your way, you are taking ownership of whatever comes your way.

Two weeks before the global pandemic shut down New York City, I took three auctions in four days for various nonprofits around the city. Standing onstage in front of hundreds of people in packed ballrooms, I had no idea that only weeks later there would be nowhere to go, nowhere to take auctions, because everything would be shut down.

In hindsight there was so much denial. We could never have imagined that so much change was coming, nor that it would alter the course of every single life in the world. Denial was a much easier emotion to process because the idea of so much change taking place at once was hard to understand, much less fathom. But looking back on 2020, the only constant in our lives was change.

Like everyone in the world, our life in 2020 changed almost overnight. Gone was the comfort of a daily routine. I desperately missed things that had at one time seemed like a chore: the simple act of getting our kids out of bed to get ready for school, making breakfast as we juggled getting ready for work, dropping them off at school, picking up coffee en route to the subway, walking into the same office where I had spent more than two decades of my life. These things vanished as we fumbled our way into our new reality. While I messaged positivity to everyone around me, inside I still felt completely uncomfortable with every element of our new normal. Instead of working with my team to create our strategy for the year, my husband and I were desperately trying to make sure that our three-, five-, and seven-year-old kids didn't miss their online classes, as well as figuring out how to send their homework to their teachers. While I was present on work calls, I always had one ear listening to one of my kids as they adjusted to their first weeks of online learning. I spent any free time left in the day navigating

Zoom updates, learning how to use Microsoft Teams, and trying to hold it all together. Gone were the days when I would torture our IT team with a question that I had always relied on them to answer. I learned how to do it on my own. It seemed like everything I did felt out of my comfort zone: setting up three children to do online learning every day, pivoting my job and my team to an online global machine overnight, not going into the office, even navigating around our beloved city where most things were shuttered. Every normal thing in our life felt like a threat: a package, the grocery store, the air that we breathed, and, worst of all, other people.

Yet in spite of this, like every other person in the world, we got out of bed every day, opened our eyes, and recalibrated to our changed lives whether or not we wanted to. We learned, we grew, our eyes were opened, and we accepted change. We learned to adapt to our new lives, to our new normal.

No matter what has happened in your life since 2020, you were forced to change. We all changed. We had no choice. In some ways, it might have been for the better, in some ways for worse, but you made it. I'll say that again, YOU MADE IT. Think back to what you didn't know before the global pandemic versus what you know now. How many ways were you able to change and move through it even if it wasn't comfortable or easy?

So, bring the confidence of making it through an unprecedented time of change to everything you do for the rest of your life. You may have fallen apart during the pandemic, you may have lost loved ones, you may have hit rock bottom, but you made it through, and you are here now. Give yourself the credit you deserve for living through a huge change and moving forward. Let that be a daily reminder that you are strong and confident enough to handle anything. When you stop expecting everything to go the way that you think it should, you put yourself in the driver's seat of your life. It's not what happens around you that matters, it's that you are strong enough to handle it and move forward.

When you realize the rules and structure you have created can change in an instant, and you can handle that change and move forward, you stop fearing change. The only constant is change, so instead of fearing it, understand that you have the ability to adapt to the change, accept it, and move through it. Change should not stop you in your tracks. Change should be something that will move you out of your comfort zone into a place where you can learn more than you knew before and allow you to bring these new skills into your ever-growing toolbox of your life.

I realized that all those years onstage learning to expect things to go wrong prepared me for this larger moment in life. Those early years of auctions when things were running late, when no one was paying attention and I had to try out anything I could think of to get the audience's attention taught me to have confidence in my ability to make things work no matter what happened. It also taught me another important lesson: much as we crave consistency and the belief that we can control everything in our lives, nothing is guaranteed. Who ever thought a global pandemic would appear and upend life as we knew it? If you looked at the top of my road map in January 2020, I wrote "write and sell your second book" at the top of the list for things I wanted to accomplish that year. I didn't write anything in

2020. I was processing so much that I had nothing left to give. But in 2021, I wrote it at the top of my road map again, and sure enough, you are reading the manifestation of that commitment.

Out of all the changes that occurred in those first months, one of the biggest changes in my work life was in charity auctioneering. I was so accustomed to the whirlwind existence of my pre-pandemic life that I desperately missed the late evenings spent onstage raising money for nonprofits. At first, like many people, I held out hope that it would be a few weeks, maybe months, before things would return to normal. By the summer of 2020, auction dates were pushed to spring 2021, and then eventually I was asked to hold dates in spring 2022.

As with most industries, the auction world went into overdrive trying to figure out how it could adapt a centuries-old auction model to fit this new virtual world. In the world of fundraising, where annual galas with hundreds of people crowded into a ballroom made up a large part of the revenue every year, a similar question was posed. How could we replicate the model of bringing people together in a room, giving them a few cocktails, and feeding off the energy to encourage them to bid?

More important, how could we make money for these non-profits? As we all realized that auctions would not be taking place for the foreseeable future, companies started coming up with solutions to address what was quickly becoming a huge issue. While the need had never been greater, the most effective model for fundraising could not happen. Some people remained overwhelmed by the unknowns around the pandemic, but others rose to meet the challenge, galvanized to fill the white space with new technology and innovation.

Two months into the pandemic I received a call from a nonprofit that wanted to try out a new virtual format for the first time. In these early stages, new software for virtual events had not been perfected, and they came up with an idea: Why not use the Zoom platform that we were all using daily for work? Since everyone was on Zoom, why not have the auction on Zoom? I listened to the call with a mixture of excitement and dread. I'll be honest, everything in me wanted to run away from this challenge. Every single fiber of my being felt resistant to this change, not to mention how worried I felt about looking absolutely ridiculous in front of hundreds of people. It is one thing to stand in front of a crowded room of people, to feed off the energy of a group of people and compel them to give more than they expect for a nonprofit. It's another thing to do that to a screen of people's faces.

On our initial call they decided that they were going to let the two hundred guests attend the auction like a Zoom meeting, and then people would raise their hands on-camera and I would take their bids one by one. As you are reading this you are probably shaking your head thinking, *This seems like a really bad idea,* and you would be right. It was a really bad idea. But at the beginning of the pandemic, there were no other options and they desperately needed to raise money, so we all agreed that this particular bad idea had to happen.

And then I did what I told you to do earlier in this chapter. I brought all the emotions I was feeling to the forefront: the anxiety, the worry, the fear of looking ridiculous. The knot in my stomach grew and grew. What was the worst case? People at home would think that I was ridiculous and spend the whole time making fun of me. Well, I couldn't see them anyway. But would we raise money? We had to be able to raise a little money for the nonprofits, so I needed to do it. But the knot didn't go away; I needed to talk it out. I called my sister and nervously explained what they wanted to do. Instead of feeding into my concerns, she started to laugh. They want you to do what? She couldn't stop laughing. I started laughing too, laughing until tears rolled down my cheeks and my sides ached. It was absolutely ludicrous—standing in my living room with two computer screens, holding an auction for hundreds of people sitting on their couches, while my kids tried to sneak in and out to grab snacks they knew they weren't supposed to have out of the kitchen. Funny. Painful but funny. She also agreed with me on one point: there was no other way to raise money as effectively, and if anyone was going to be able to do it, it should be someone who had already been through the worst-case auction scenarios possible. Me. It's not like I haven't fallen flat on my face before—school auction without a microphone, anyone?

When I get onstage at this point in my career, there are few things that you can throw at me that I have not seen. My arsenal for last-minute issues and changes is vast because of the years I have spent recovering from anything and everything you can think of. We've covered the lack of microphone, but there have been so many others: drunk guest gets onstage and tries to commandeer the microphone, man has a stroke right before the auction and the ambulance comes mid-auction with sirens and lights blaring, woman is overserved and bids too much only to yell out "I can't pay for that" when she realizes that she has won. Every time one of these things happened, I would feel completely shaken and get offstage feeling like the entire evening was ruined. How could I have let that person talk for so long? Why didn't I do this instead of that? But as the years have passed, I realized that these experiences have taught me how to be nimble.

When I get onstage at an auction and everything goes right, it seems like an outlier. More often than not, a curveball is thrown somewhere over the course of the night and I have to course correct to ensure that the audience doesn't have any idea that something that was not supposed to happen has happened. But I don't let myself fall into the thinking that dominated my early years, where I questioned everything I did when something didn't go the way we thought it would. Instead, I learned to be confident enough to know that when I stepped on that stage, I was bringing all those years of experience, changes, and mistakes along with me. If things didn't go well, it was an opportunity for growth—something I could improve in future auctions.

After two months of discussions and tech rehearsals, auction day arrived. In order to troubleshoot any potential issues that could arise, the nonprofit had sent a computer via FedEx for the auction. I spent an hour assembling all the new equipment in the package: a high-tech microphone, a ring light, and a computer. I gathered a variety of different items around my house to ensure that I was eye level with the screen. (I'll be honest, at five eleven, it took a little while to gather enough items to make it high enough to meet my eye.) We held a run-through the day before to ensure that we all knew what we were doing. After a semi-successful run-through, we agreed that I would get online exactly one hour prior to the event the next evening so that we could review everything one last time.

The night of the auction I stood in front of my closet trying to figure out what to wear. After much deliberation I chose a cocktail dress and a pair of heels. I remember laughing as I put on the heels. The camera only showed an image from the shoulders up, but I still wanted to feel like I was showing up to go onstage instead of twenty feet from my kitchen. After a couple of quick camera checks, I realized that the important thing wasn't the dress, it was a statement necklace or big earrings. New gig, new uniform. Change is the name of the game. I changed my dress into a top and stood in front of the computer, ready for this new world. But, of course, I wore the heels anyway.

If I had a master's degree in dealing with the unexpected from so many years as a charity auctioneer, my first night as a virtual charity auctioneer gave me a PhD. Gone overnight was the identity I had spent seventeen years creating—the tall, sassy auctioneer in a brightly colored cocktail dress onstage in front of hundreds, commanding the stage with the energy of a packed ballroom. I was no longer an auctioneer with a live audience; I was a woman on a computer screen in her living room. It was hard to remember what it felt like to stride confidently onstage when I felt like my life was held together with duct tape and Popsicle sticks. If you had looked in the window of my apartment on the night of an auction, you would have seen that statement in physical form. The computer I used for auctions was leaning precariously off a pile of books and various boxes from around my apartment to make it eye level while I used my husband's computer as a makeshift teleprompter.

Exactly an hour before the start of the auction, I called in to the conference line they had set up, so we had an open line during the event. As I chatted with the event organizer, I turned on the computer and pulled up the link that they had sent to access the auction platform. I double clicked the new link and waited while the computer scrolled and scrolled before an error message displayed on the screen. I clicked the link again since we had rehearsed this exact moment the day before. But unlike the day before, the Zoom link didn't open up. It scrolled and scrolled and gave another error message. I pressed it again and the same thing happened.

You know that feeling when everything seems to be totally fine and then you get a sinking feeling that everything is not going to be fine? That was how I felt at that exact moment. In a regular auction setting, there are event organizers who can troubleshoot in real time with the audiovisual team. But in this new virtual world, the event was being streamed from Colorado, so there was no one to help me in my apartment in New York.

As the minutes ticked by, I started feeling seriously panicked by my lack of control of the situation. No one on the team seemed to know what to do, so they put a young woman on the phone that they had appointed the "tech lead." I could tell from her nervous energy that this was a promotion she had received shortly before I called with my first question. As we neared the event start time, I could see the director of the nonprofit pacing in his studio as we tried different solutions to make it work.

Not only was I nervous that we weren't going to figure out how to get onto the auction, but I was also incredibly anxious about the fact that I was going to be taking a Zoom auction with two hundred people for the first time in my life. Eight minutes before the auction we finally figured it out: the computer they sent me for the auction, the one that had been FedExed to my home specifically for the sole purpose of the auction, had not been updated with the latest software. The minute I saw the Zoom icon download, I felt my knees go weak. A quick software update and we were ready to go. I was already exhausted from the hour spent trying to figure out how to make the computer work.

I felt the stress in my body as the minutes ticked by until the start of the auction. The voices on our shared conference line counted me down *"Three, two, one . . ."* and I was on. Twenty-five Zoom boxes filled my screen with a tab indicating that there were eight more pages of Zoom boxes. I gave everyone a smile and quickly introduced myself, feeling completely uncertain. On a stage with my gavel I feel fearless, confident in my ability, but on a camera in my living room I felt none of those things. As you all probably know from Zoom, no one simply stares into their camera when there are a lot of people on a Zoom call. I could see people drinking a glass of wine, people on mute chatting with each other, empty Zoom boxes, and even one woman—smack in the middle of my screen—who was desperately trying to get something out from between her two front teeth.

My first instinct was to laugh out loud. What an absolute mess. I could only see twenty-five of the two hundred attendees; everyone looked as confused as I felt. As I introduced myself, I did the only thing I could think of in that moment: I spoke the truth. But first, the gavel strike.

"Ladies and gentlemen, I want to thank you all so much for showing up this evening. I know that this is a foreign concept to all of us—this is the first auction I have ever taken on Zoom. We have a plan for how this is supposed to go, but as we all know from the past couple of months, change is the name of the game. If you can't figure out how to bid, know that anything goes. I will make it work, and we will figure it out together." I took a deep breath.

"If you need to take yourself off mute and tell me your name and bid amount, I will take it. And if you can't figure out how to unmute yourself, I am going to give you the event director's phone number and you can text him that information." And that is exactly what we did. We took bids from the chat function, people yelled out money, teenagers popped into the screen to bid for their parents. I felt lucky that no one had anywhere else to be, the one benefit of a global pandemic, so they sat patiently as I cracked jokes and we figured it out on the fly. From a performance standpoint, if I'm honest, it was a total mess. But there was something so incredible about that moment, because despite the fact that it was a mess, we raised a lot of money that evening. We were all forced to change, but we adapted as we needed to keep moving forward.

When I logged off, I was relieved, but also incredibly proud. Proud that I tried something that felt so uncomfortable when many of my fellow charity auctioneers had flatly refused to try out a virtual program. Was it great? No. Would the next one be better? The bar was so low the answer had to be yes. The most important thing was that it proved, once again, that pushing through that fear of the unknown, that fear of change, forces you to grow. It gives you the confidence to walk into a room.

Over the next year and a half of virtual evenings, every time I started working with a new group I would tell them the same thing: "The one thing I can promise you is that something will go wrong tonight. We don't know what it is, but something unexpected *will* happen." When I saw their faces turn red or they started to get flustered, I would say what I truly believed, what I knew from experiencing it firsthand: "We'll get through it and it will be fine." It turns out I was right.

There was only one auction in eighteen months where everything went seamlessly. One auction out of thirty-two auctions. The only reason for that perfect performance was that I was on-site at a sound studio where a team worked to ensure it was flawless. Otherwise, something did go wrong at every auction: the bidding software didn't work, videos didn't play, the entire program froze and had to be restarted five minutes later, bidders didn't understand the technology and started making comments about it in the chat box during the auction. I learned from each of those moments, as did everyone around me. We changed, we learned, we grew from the experience, and we all gained confidence in ourselves and these newfound skills that we never knew that we would need or want in our lifetime.

Life is an ever-evolving conversation in which change is the only constant. To be at the top of your game, you need to embrace change and realize that *you* are the constant in the ever-changing game. When you are steady, unflappable, and always at the ready, you will have claimed your confidence and you will be ready to take on anything and everything that comes your way.

CHERI LEAVY & WHITNEY LONG

Cofounders of The Southern Coterie

The older we get, as we grow both personally and profession-ally, we realize that change is inevitable. Oftentimes it comes down to our mindset—do we embrace it or fight it? And while change can be a little scary, intimidating, or uncomfortable, change defines and refines us. View change as opportunities to pivot. Pivots aren't failures—frame it as progression. And don't be afraid of failure, anyway—it is during these times that we learn lessons as we grow. Look at being nimble and embracing change as taking advantage of new opportunities and innova-tions. We always strive to listen to the needs of our members so we can serve them where they are, as they grow and change. We know firsthand that as entrepreneurs, change is the only constant!

12

YOU ARE FINE

Have you ever heard a story that sticks with you like glue? At the time, you don't know why it resonates so deeply, but it comes to mind constantly over the days and weeks that follow. And then a few days or maybe a few months or years later, something monumental happens in your life and you realize there was a reason you heard that story, and at the same it becomes crystal clear that everything in your life has been leading to this moment. A moment that required years of training your mind and body to believe that you have the confidence to handle anything, no matter how challenging or difficult.

A few years ago, I was sitting at a party when a friend of mine launched into a story about ultramarathoning. She would be the first to tell you she has never owned a pair of running shoes, and likely would only run if there was a flash sale at Bergdorf Goodman, but she was so floored by what she heard that she felt compelled to share the message. The story was about ultramarathoners—elite runners who train their bodies and minds to run 50, 100, 200 miles without stopping. The runners were talking about the moment in the race where their bodies hit a wall, depleted of energy, calories, or anything that would allow a mere mortal to continue running. When they hit the point when their mind began to play tricks on them, pushing them to the brink, they would inevitably tell their partners they were done. Enough. Time to give up. Instead of leaving them behind, their running partners would look them square in the eyes and repeat, "You are fine. You are fine," almost rhythmically. The runner would repeat back to them, "I am fine. I am fine," until their mind took over and brought them back to a place where they could continue with the race. The story fascinated me. The thought that even if your body is depleted of everything, when you have hit a wall that should make it impossible to move on, your mind can carry you forward.

As I am an eternal optimist, this story appealed to me on many levels. As you know from reading this book, I believe that mindset and positivity are critical elements in living a confident life. I also believe we have the ability to control the outcome of everything we do in our life, no matter what is shifting around us. I believe that applies to living in the moment as much as it applies to how we think about the future, how we set goals, and how we move toward goals. To me, the future has always been something that seems completely abstract. I know that it exists and that we are moving toward it every day, yet it also feels very far away. When I think about my future, I see it as a road stretching out for miles and miles in front of me.

There are parts of the future that I avoid thinking about too much: my parents aging, getting older, my kids leaving and starting their own lives. Yet there are so many things that excite me about the future: the boundless opportunities, trips to countries in the world I haven't seen, the unfulfilled potential of life just waiting to be fulfilled. Perhaps it is that I am an eternal optimist, but it truly never occurred to me that in one moment there could be no future.

As we buckled our kids into their seats on the evening of October 31, 2021, I certainly wasn't thinking about our future or anything other than trying to find any small stashes of candy my kids might have hidden in their Halloween costumes. I was pretty sure that I could find some loose contraband in their pockets that they were planning to stuff in their mouths as we drove back to Manhattan. Sure enough, I heard them squeal in dismay as I found a few pieces, confiscated them, and put them in my pocket. My husband limped toward the driver's side, his leg still stiff from a ruptured Achilles tendon injury from the summer. As I closed the trunk, I thought how convenient it would be that I could dump the candy bags in the trash after dropping our car off at our parking garage when we arrived back in the city. I could then pretend that we had left them in the trunk and voilà! By the next time we used the car they would likely have forgotten about it altogether.

We had spent Halloween trick-or-treating with friends in a suburb outside of New York City, choosing the ease of a suburban trick-or-treating experience to the chaos of a NYC Halloween. I love the experience of raising kids in the city, but there is also something fun about showing them that there is a different way to live. Judging by the increasingly loud protests from the kids over their lost candy, I could tell that this wasn't going to be the most fun hour drive back to the city, nor was bedtime likely to be easy, given the hundred pieces of candy they had probably eaten within the hour.

A light rain was falling as we said goodbye to our friends and pulled out of the driveway, our headlights illuminating the kids running back and forth from house to house in search of more candy. As we pulled onto the road, our kids continued to talk about their Halloween loot, discussing which houses had given full-sized candy bars instead of the minis. The conversation inevitably turned back to my Halloween loot confiscation, and I knew that a full mutiny was only minutes away. I searched through my phone to find something that would distract them, finally settling on a story time podcast that I hoped would keep them quiet for at least part of the drive home. I found a suitable story, hit play, and within minutes a quiet calm had settled over our car. I glanced behind me and saw them quietly staring out their windows into the dark night except for my oldest daughter, who had closed her eyes. I settled into my seat and typed in the web address for the *New York Post*. An image of the White House press secretary flashed up with the headline PRESS SECRETARY JEN PSAKI HAS CORONAVIRUS. *That's a pretty green dress*, I thought. That is the last thing I remember before the world went black.

I don't remember the first thing that I remember because I felt like I was being pulled out of a dream in slow motion. I remember sound, muffled, my kids screaming. I struggled for air. My entire body felt numb, almost lifeless. I opened my eyes and groaned, trying to find the breath to reassure my children before realizing there was no breath, only gasping for air. My eyes were trying to make sense of what was in front of me. Our windshield was no longer a windshield but rather a spiderweb of cracks, grotesquely misshapen. The dashboard was no longer an organized display of lights and numbers, but rather a mess of deployed airbags and wrong angles. As I tried to focus, I realized that my left eye was completely blurry; it was as if I was looking through the lens of a kaleidoscope instead of the clear vision that I have relied on my entire life. Still not comprehending what happened, I continued to try to find the words to reassure my kids, but the wind had been knocked out of me so completely by the air bag that I could barely muster a whisper. My head was slumped back on the left side of the head rest, and I could see my husband completely still, eyes closed in the driver's seat next to me. Moments later he stirred and then cried out.

I barely whispered, "Chris. Oh my God. Oh my God. What happened?"

His voice sounded as weak as mine. "A car was flying through the air . . ."

I watched as Chris, boosted by a surge of adrenaline, sat upright and pushed open his car door. I felt the air rush in, lights from the opposite highway flashing by as he opened the car door to see the middle seat of the car where all three kids sat side by side crying and screaming. *"Mommy, Mommy, Daddy."* I tried to get up, to move, but I felt pinned down by the weight of a body; I couldn't move no matter what my mind was telling me. My chest felt like it had been hit so hard I could barely breathe. The kids?

Their screams came back into focus. I closed my eyes and tried to listen for each of the kids—to make sure I could hear each of their voices screaming, so at the very least I knew they were alive. I heard Chris reassuring the kids before disappearing again. The next thing I knew my car door was opening and Chris was there, cradling his left arm but reassuring me that the kids were okay, while trying to help me get out. Everything in my mind was telling me to move, but my body would not cooperate. I was in a world of something. Pain? Numbness? I was still gasping for air, taking shallow breaths because that was all my body would allow. It was such a strange feeling, not being able to breathe in or command my body to move. Everything in me wanted to get out and clutch each of my babies in my arms, but physically I could not sit up, turn around to see my kids, or move my body out of the car. It felt broken. Everything was broken.

"Please, Chris, please, I can't move. Don't move me. Are the kids okay?"

Chris was clutching his arm to his side. "I think they're okay. They're all okay." He moved to the back to help the kids out of the car.

As they started to get out, I tried to call out to them with any breath I could muster. "Are you guys okay? Mommy's okay." They couldn't hear me.

"I love you. I love you." I tried to make noise but there was no air. My voice was nothing but a whisper.

One by one the kids got out of the car, still crying. As they left the car the silence was deafening, interrupted only by the online vehicle security system—who informed me that an ambulance had been called. As I felt my breath slowly come back, the representative's voice kept me from passing out from the pain.

"Ma'am, can you tell me your name?"

"Lydia Fenet," I whispered.

"How many people are in the vehicle?"

I focused on answering his questions instead of thinking about what was happening. "Five. There are five of us, but my husband took my kids out, so I am the only one left in the car." I tried to focus on the filtered light coming through the spiderweb of cracked glass that had once been our windshield.

My door opened again as a Good Samaritan looked in. "Are you okay?"

"Yes. I'm okay. I can't move but I'm okay."

He looked shell-shocked. "The ambulance is coming. Just hang in there." He left the door open, and I heard him encouraging the driver of the car that had flown through the air and collided with ours. Two separate stories colliding in one tragic moment. I could tell from the urgency in his voice that she was not doing well.

"You've got this. You're a warrior. I'm here with you. I'm here. Don't you leave me. You're a fighter." He repeated this, his voice filled with so much emotion. I closed my eyes. I prayed. How had this happened? We had been trick-or-treating twenty minutes ago. Our kids were still in their costumes. I prayed. Prayed for the driver, for my family, my parents, my husband, my children. I tried to start the Lord's Prayer that I had said so many times throughout my life, but every time I would start to pray, my mind would wander. My parents, my siblings, Chris, my kids. How had this happened?

———

I don't know how long it took for the ambulances to arrive, but in that quiet car the time seemed endless. At the time, I had no idea that minutes later the firemen and EMTs would arrive to cut me out of the car and put me on a stretcher. I had no idea what was going on outside the car, what was going to happen, what was happening.

I couldn't see anything except for the windshield and the blood that was all over my face from a wound above my left eyebrow. I so badly needed to reframe this narrative. I was alive. Was I blind in my left eye? Maybe. That was bad, but there were worse things. My body? I moved my feet, my hands. I remembered watching the pilot for *Friday Night Lights* when the main character sustained a spinal injury. He couldn't feel his fingers or toes. I could. I could move them both. Maybe I wasn't paralyzed. But mentally I went there. Okay. Paralyzed. You'll be okay. You will be fine. You will be fine. You are alive, Chris is alive, your kids are alive. You will be fine.

After what seemed like an eternity, the back door of the car opened, and I heard an unfamiliar voice. "Lydia? Lydia?"

"Yes," I whispered, my head still slumped back on the shoulder of my seat.

"I'm Daniella."

I stretched my hand backward and she took it with both hands.

"I want to let you know that I have your children in my car. They are bruised pretty badly and I think they have a few broken bones, but they are alive. They are all talking. They want to know if you are okay."

I squeezed her hand, felt tears welling up in my eyes. I realized I hadn't cried until that moment. "Yes. I am okay. Thank you so much. Thank you for being here."

"They are watching a movie and I'll be with them until the ambulance arrives." I was numb. Numb with pain. Numb from emotion. Numb.

The ambulances could have taken three minutes to arrive or thirty minutes to arrive. After Daniella left, I remember closing my eyes and listening for the sirens, faintly at first, and then louder and louder until they were right outside the car. The stillness and quiet of the car were interrupted abruptly. Firemen and EMTs surrounded the car. Suddenly there was a flashlight in my eyes, checking my pupils, my wrist outstretched as someone checked my pulse. "What's your name? Ma'am, what's your name?"

"Lydia Fenet."

Over the next few minutes, they debated how to get me out of the car as they cut away at airbags and other pieces of the car in an effort to smooth my way out. Then I was heaved out of the back door onto a stretcher and loaded into an ambulance. Suddenly, my body was convulsing so badly I could barely stay on the stretcher. My body was in shock, but my mind was still present. I struggled to say my name as my body continued to shake.

"She's going into shock again," someone said. I closed my eyes.

Minutes later the ambulance pulled into the ER and I felt the doors open as the stretcher was pulled out. Doctors swarmed around me, poking, prodding. I felt the tugging of my clothes as they cut them off my body, a moment of levity when I heard the doctors laugh as my down puffer was cut and feathers filled the air. Then the pain of needles sticking my body everywhere and medical terms that I had only heard on TV being thrown around—cat scan, fractured ribs, broken spine, internal bleeding. After what seemed like an eternity, I was wheeled out of the ER and into a room that was set off to the side.

"Lydia? Lydia? Can you hear me?" I opened my eyes. "We are going to bring your family in here to see you. They are all here—all of them." The words I had been waiting to hear. I strained from my neck brace to see them all walk in. I wasn't prepared for what came next. The last time I saw my husband he was reassuring me by the side of the car, and from what Daniella said when she was in my car, I assumed my children were walking around and were all fine.

Out of the corner of my eye I saw a line of stretchers being wheeled in by attendants. First Chris, in unbelievable pain, his arm wrapped and bound against his body, trying to catch a breath from what he would find out was a shattered wrist. Then my little Eloise clutching her little broken arm, looking pale as a ghost; followed by Henry and Beatrice in neck braces, lying in shock. I held back tears as I heard "MOMMY MOMMY MOMMY MOMMY."

It took everything in me not to throw up as they lined us all up next to one another on stretchers. I felt my breath catch, thinking that it could have easily been the five of us lined up in a morgue. But we weren't dead. We were alive. We were all so very alive. All of us.

One by one the kids started to cry, and the nurses moved their beds in a rotation, so I could hold their hands.

As the stretchers rolled in, I saw something else. Coming in with the stretchers were my father-in-law, mother-in-law, sister-in-law, and sister whom Chris had called from the accident. All of a sudden I realized that what we had experienced was only the beginning. There was also the fear and shock of our families who had almost lost a son, daughter, and their only grandchildren/nieces and nephews in one instant. I have no doubt they knew it was bad when they first received the call, but nothing could have prepared them for what they saw in that room that evening.

In that moment, in that bright fluorescent lighting, lying on a stretcher next to my family, I thanked God that we were together in pain instead of the alternative. And I realized that no matter how much pain I was in, no matter how hard this was for me, I needed to be the rock for my children. To show them what I had learned about life in the years leading up to this moment. I knew whatever came next was going to be hard and painful, but the smaller moments that had challenged me throughout my life, powering my positivity, never giving up and getting knocked down had prepared me to weather this storm.

I was in a neck brace with a fractured spine, seven fractured ribs, and a large gash on my forehead, and in fifteen minutes I would be going in for internal surgery because they were concerned I had internal bleeding and was bleeding to death. I didn't know any of that. I just knew that what I said at that moment mattered to everyone. The story of the ultramarathoners came flooding back to me. No matter what happened, we would be fine. As long as we were alive, we were fine. If I said it, my kids would believe it. If I said it, everyone else would take their cue from that message.

My voice must have gone up two octaves. "My sweet babies. Don't cry. We are all together and we are going to be FINE. We are the strongest family in the world. We are going to be fine. Okay? I promise. Mommy is here, Daddy is here, Bebe and Ba, Aunt Hilary, and Aunt Katelyn are here, and we are all going to be FINE. I know that was super scary, it was so so scary, but we made it through the worst part and are all going to be FINE. We are going to be so good. The doctors and nurses will take care of us and put us all back together and soon we can all go home, but right now the most important thing to remember is that we are going to be okay. Okay?" They nodded tearfully.

As if on cue, each of them started to talk about the accident. Just as Chris and I had such different experiences with the accident, the kids had seen different things and had different questions. Beatrice's question broke my heart. "Why didn't you answer us when we called you, Mommy? We thought you were dead." Henry voiced the same concern.

My heart broke, but I also needed to be honest. "Mommy was unconscious from the air bag. I was trying to talk, but my voice wasn't loud enough."

Eloise's biggest concern was about the car, which she feared was in really bad shape. She wasn't wrong. The car was completely mangled, the front of it unrecognizable. But her comment that came later was the one that I will never forget as long as I live. For Halloween, Eloise had picked out the costume of Supergirl and, as the youngest child, was always fighting for something. As her brother and sister continued to talk, Eloise voiced her thoughts loudly over the other two: "Mommy, Mommy, I used my superpowers to stop the car. I saved us all."

Henry immediately shot her down: "No you didn't, Eloise. You don't have superpowers!"

"YES, I DO," she roared back. There was something so comforting about hearing them act like siblings even when they were on stretchers in a hospital.

"Lydia. We need to take you to the OR immediately." Minutes later I was rolled into the operating room for internal surgery. There was significant fluid in my pelvis, and the doctors expressed concern that my internal organs were ruptured. They were going to perform internal surgery to make sure that I wasn't bleeding to death. "We are going to go in and we'll just have to start cutting out any of your organs that are dying," the doctor said as I signed a massive pile of waivers. As they pushed me through the waiting room leading to the OR, I saw the concerned faces of the OR staff, the ER staff, everyone who had come to aid a family of five who was living their worst nightmare. But I didn't want them to be sad or to pity me. What had I just told me family? We were fine. I was fine. Deep down I knew it. Even if everything internally was not okay, I would be okay no matter what happened. The coming weeks and months would be painful, but I needed them to understand that I wasn't broken in spirit, even if my body felt differently.

"You guys look so serious. I'm going to be great. All I need you to focus on is making sure that I am ready to be back in a bathing suit for summer, so make sure those scars are teeny."

The surgeon laughed. "Okay. I can see you just had a birthday—"

"Yes," I interjected, "but subtract twenty years from that and let's just go with that number for now."

He laughed again. The atmosphere that had felt so stifling and so tense dissipated. I felt normal again. In control of my own narrative. Even with a broken body, I knew that I was strong. All those years training my body and mind had made me confident that this was something I could move through and ultimately overcome.

Pain or no pain. Car wreck or no car wreck. I was not about to wallow in self-pity. I needed to mentally prepare myself for what was coming next. That would not happen if I went to rock bottom and stayed there. There would be plenty of time to reflect on what happened, but for now it was about maintaining a positive attitude with everyone around me and repeating it until I believed it more than anyone else around me. To reframe the narrative.

I woke up in a hospital room hours later with my sister by my side. The pain was unbelievable. There was nothing on my body that didn't hurt. My sister held my hand, tears in her eyes as she told me that the children had been admitted to the hospital along with my husband. Hilary became the calm in the storm in the days that followed. The conductor, the organizer, the gatekeeper, the everything. She assured me that my kids were as fine as they could be under the circumstances. My youngest daughter had suffered a fractured arm, my son and oldest daughter were both covered in bone bruises and cuts from the seat belts that had saved their lives. My in-laws and younger brother were each sleeping in a room with a different child, to ensure there was someone with them nonstop. Over the next few days my sister would move between my room and their rooms as they received a battery of tests and images. But that night, the nurse ushered my sister out of the room, leaving me alone.

It wasn't my first time in the hospital. I had a C-section with my oldest daughter and two other natural births, so I knew what to expect over the course of the night. The next few hours were a blur of doctors, nurses, shots, temperature checks, and painkillers. The pain was unfathomable. My body hurt everywhere. There was nothing that didn't hurt. I looked at the clock, willing the minutes to pass, trying to focus on my belief that with each minute that passed I might feel a little better. In the wee hours of the morning, it occurred to me that I should probably let my team know I would not be showing up to the office that day or any day in the near future. Half-delirious from the surgery, I texted my boss and my team a short email letting them know what was going on. After I finished the email, I cut and pasted the text to a few friends, letting them know what had happened so that they could inform anyone who heard about the accident. Mercifully the pain medication kicked in, and then everything went black.

After only a few hours I woke up to the trauma team standing at the foot of my bed talking about the extent of my injuries. The internal surgery had confirmed that my internal organs were fine, but my ribs were cracked and fractured on both sides. I would need spinal surgery to repair my lower spine in the coming days, but I was not paralyzed. I would be able to walk and, in time, run again. They realized my husband was only four rooms down and moved me into his room where we both lay in hospital beds. We made quite a pair, to say the least. My sister sat in a chair between us, there to anticipate anything we needed, but quite frankly, we were both in too much pain to do anything except sleep.

A few hours after I arrived in the room, Chris picked up his phone. "Lydia, how do so many people know about the accident? I have so many texts." My sister had plugged my phone in across the room, so I hadn't looked at it since I had been moved into the room. My sister unplugged the phone and brought it back to the bed. I stared at my phone—my voicemail was full, there were hundreds of texts, emails, and DMs on Instagram. The text messages that I had sent at 4:30 a.m. had spread like wildfire. They had been forwarded and forwarded and shared and texted to seemingly every person I'd ever met.

Over the next few days, our community rallied around us with a ferocity of love that was truly unfathomable. It was like a tidal wave that continued to pick up speed every minute of every hour of every day. While my parents flew in and my mom moved into my room, my sister moved between the pediatric ward and my room, keeping me abreast of everything that was happening with our children. My mom and my sister did everything that I could no longer do; the simple act of reaching my arm out to get water hurt so badly I couldn't bring myself to do it. The day after the accident, I woke up in a fog of medication and pain and heard the voices of my closest friends in my room. Despite the fact that my family told them not to show up, they didn't stay away. I couldn't have been more grateful that they refused the request. It felt like we were living two lives—they were dressed, talking about what they were doing later in the day and even later that week. I couldn't move and had forgotten in such a short amount of time what life was like outside of my hospital bed.

Extended family and friends moved between the children's ward and the room that Chris and I shared, telling funny stories about the kids, bringing treats, and giving encouragement when we needed it. The nurses eventually turned a blind eye to the fact that I seemed to have a never-ending stream of "sisters" who looked nothing like me or each other. Chris and I were never alone, and the kids had family and friends with them at all times. Late at night when the nurses would come in to check my blood pressure, administer blood thinners, or give me pain medication, each of them confided that what I had experienced was their worst nightmare—and the worst nightmare of doctors and nurses in any trauma center. We were beyond lucky to have lived, they all told me, because they had seen so many families that had not been as lucky. I took comfort in the hospital chaplain who stopped by every day to ask if we needed anything. We prayed each day for our family and for everyone else involved in the accident.

On the days when the pain was so intense I could barely breathe, my best friends followed the nurses around until they came up with a pain management system that meant I could actually open my eyes instead of spending all of my time hiding under the sheet, clenched up, trying to make it from minute to minute. As each day passed, they showed up with more and more—flowers, food, nail polish, hairbrushes, robes, socks, anything they could think of to make me feel like a normal person. And even more than that, they showed up for my children. They covered them with love, with presents, with hugs and kisses. I called downstairs to talk to the nurse in charge of Eloise one day, only to be told laughingly that she kept escaping her room for her brother's and sister's rooms. The only way they could find her was from the glitter of her mermaid costume and the Oreo crumb trail, as she had been eating Oreos nonstop since she arrived. It was overwhelming and incredible to know this community of people would do whatever it took to make sure that we would be okay. Our bodies would need to heal, our minds to process what had happened, but we would be fine.

Our community gave us the strength, courage, and love that we needed to bolster us up, but ultimately the act of healing our bodies and moving forward was not something anyone else could do. That work had to be done by us. It's easy to blame other people, to be angry for circumstances that are beyond our control, but only we control our mindset, our attitude, how we respond and frame the narrative of our story and our lives. We are all Eloise. We all possess a superpower in life. All of us. But it's only when we stop looking around for other people to save us that we gain the greatest gift: the ability to inspire other people, to bring positivity to the darkest moments, to overcome, to grow, and to live. My spinal surgery was scheduled for seven o'clock on a Wednesday morning, but because of the number of traumas that came in that day, the OR wasn't available until 1:30 a.m. the next morning. As the attendant wheeled me down the empty, darkened hallway in the middle of the night to the OR where I had been rushed in only four days before with my entire family, I saw the OR attendant who had been there the night I was wheeled in.

As she came over to speak with me about the upcoming operation, she stopped. "Are you the mom who came in with her kids on Halloween after the car wreck?" Even though we were both wearing masks because of Covid, I could see the smile in her eyes.

"We are all good. My kids left yesterday. I'm doing well."

She laughed. "Doing well? That isn't usually what people say when they come here about to get a spinal fusion. I'll tell you something, I knew you would be okay the night you came here because you had such a positive attitude. We all talked about how you were making jokes when everything was so bad. I've worked here over twenty years and I see forty-year-olds go in for surgery with a bad attitude who don't make it, and I see eighty-year-olds who come in here with a positive attitude and have no reason to live walk out of here with no problem. You are going to be fine because you believe you are going to be fine."

It was an affirmation of everything I knew to be true, what I knew in my heart, what I had seen in my own life, and what I needed to hear that night. Something to pass along to anyone reading this who feels like they are not up to the challenge. You will be fine. You have the power to overcome the most difficult challenges if you believe and trust yourself to be fine. Believe it and your body will follow.

After eight days, I returned home to the same apartment I had lived in before the accident, but nothing felt the same. Everything was the same, but my ability to move around and do anything was decidedly not. No bending over meant I couldn't pick up anything I dropped, getting in and out of bed was no longer easy because my fractured ribs made it difficult to sit up, and my fused spine made it difficult to get up. Even laughter was off-limits because it hurt to laugh; I spent as much time yelling at my sister to stop making me laugh as she did running out of my room trying to keep from laughing. My mother moved in to help with the kids, and without her I don't know what we would have done. She cared for us and comforted us and opened the door for the flowers and food and gifts that arrived almost every minute of every day. Chris's wrist surgery meant that he couldn't use his left hand, and with all of my restrictions, we joked that between us we made up exactly three-quarters of one person.

As someone who has thrived on living a life on fast forward, it took work to slow down. To sleep. To do less and accept help more. To give my body the grace it deserved to recover from trauma. In many ways I had no choice. Whether or not I wanted to slow down, my body would simply shut down. I accepted any and every offer from anyone who offered anything. My younger brother was a constant presence—playing with my kids in the apartment, taking them to the park. My in-laws had taken my kids home when they were discharged from the hospital and had cared for them until I was ready to go home. Friends would drop by for five minutes to say hi. As I grew stronger, they would stop by and walk me around the block. They texted, called, DMed, offered to pick up the kids. I knew that to stay strong and positive I needed to draw from the energy of the people around me, to accept from the community and friends

I have spent my life investing in. When it all seemed too much, when the pain was too intense, or the recovery seemed like it would never end, I would stare in the mirror and repeat, "I am fine. I am fine. I am fine." And I was. It wasn't that the pain wasn't there, it was. It wasn't that the recovery was or is easy, it wasn't, and it still isn't, but by keeping myself in a mental state where I constantly focused on the positive and moving forward, I never looked back and said, "What if this hadn't happened?" Rather, I looked forward and thought, *What will I be able to do next week that I couldn't do last week?*

Days after the accident a friend of mine sat next to me holding my hand as I tried to find any slightly comfortable position in my hospital bed. She burst into tears. "I'm so angry. Why did this happen to you? You are such a good person and you are such a good family. Why? Why did this happen?"

My reaction was so fast it surprised me. "Why not? Why not me?" Anger was never an emotion that came to me at any time during the hospital or the days afterward. Sadness, pain, hope, gratitude, exhaustion, elation, yes. But anger, never. No one has a perfect life. There is no such thing. When we expect that we deserve something from life, that we are deserving of a certain type of life, we lose sight of the most important fact: Life itself is a gift. All of it.

Every day that I choose to get out of bed and work hard at recovery, I show my kids what it means to show up for life. I know that throughout their lives they will be stronger because they watched their father and mother overcome this difficult experience and keep moving forward. Even at their young ages they have been tested and persevered. My four-year-old might have been the toughest one of all, back in school with a broken arm the week after the accident as if nothing had happened to her.

For me, this accident brought something else into focus. The fragility of life. The beauty of life. The life that we all get to live— in the highs and the lows. When I was sitting in the car not knowing what the future would hold, there was one thing that was certain. I wanted to live. To be alive. To experience more, to see more, to spend more time with those around me and those I have yet to meet. I want to watch my kids grow up, grow old with my husband, take care of my parents as they get older, write more books, and continue to reach for goals every day for the rest of my life. This accident also gave me an unexpected gift. I didn't realize when you have experienced such intense trauma, people in your life and complete strangers open up to you about things they have experienced that changed them. People I have known a long time confided in me about car accidents they were in as children; people told me about beating cancer, losing family members unexpectedly. A woman I had never met reached out a week before her spinal surgery over Instagram and I supported her from afar as she recovered from her surgery. The shared human experience is what life is about, and it has been incredible to be trusted with this from so many people.

———————

There were so many lessons that this accident taught me, and so many things I want to pass along to you. First and foremost, I want to say thank you. Thank you for going on this journey with me. It is a privilege and a joy to write these words for you. I hope that you will choose the lessons that speak to you or that some phrase or story in this book will inspire you to become the architect of your life and go after your dreams with confidence.

What I want for each and every one of you is to learn from what I experienced. I glimpsed what could have happened if Halloween 2021 had been my last day on earth. I can honestly tell you that I had no regrets. I have lived the life I wanted, feeling the low of every low and the high of every high. There is such freedom, such release in knowing that.

———

I want to leave you with this. Live your life for you. Be confident in the words and the actions that you put out there and unafraid to go after whatever you want in life. Today. We don't all get second chances. We don't all get the opportunity to keep living the life we create, so make yourself proud. Untether yourself from what other people think about you. Stop letting the fear of the unknown or other people's ideas keep you from living your life.

Surround yourself with a community of people who are there for you in the good but also in the worst possible times. Right now, today, this very moment, if you don't love your life, I want you to change it. Not to think about changing it, but to change it. Because trust me when I say it can all be gone tomorrow. Have the confidence to change if you don't love it and find the confidence to believe in yourself starting right now.

Over the course of your life there will be moments when you

think you can't go on. You can. There will be moments when you want to give in. You won't. You have all the confidence you need to go after whatever you want inside you. Don't be scared of it; don't fear it; embrace it, because no matter what happens, you will be fine.

I hope that you read this story and it sticks with you like glue. A story that you can't shake no matter how hard you try. And the next time you are facing something that pushes you to your limit, when you think can't go on in whatever you are facing, you can hear these words: You are fine. Know it. Believe it to your core. And live your life to the fullest.

Claim your confidence. No one deserves to feel more confident than you. It's time to go out there and get the life you deserve.

EPILOGUE

ALL OR NOTHING

I am writing these words on the last day of 2021. The final days of the year are meant to let us close the door on the past and move forward into the future with a hope for brighter things to come. We all did that in 2020, hopeful that the global pandemic would be over and life would return to normal. Or what was normal. Yet 2021 turned out to be nothing like we expected. Instead, it was a year filled with the unexpected and even more unexpected. A year we thought would see the end of the global pandemic only to find out that it would come roaring back time and time again.

Almost two years have passed since we all began this journey, and though they were difficult, we should all be grateful for the lessons we have learned. We have been faced with enormous change and adversity that few of us ever thought we would live to see. Through all the ups and downs I believe what I wrote in this book now more than ever. When you choose to claim your confidence and take ownership of the decisions in your life, the shifting uncertainties of life become the backdrop of your life story. They no longer define you because you no longer fear the unknown. You have prepared for it, trained for it, and you know that anything is possible when you have the confidence to believe you can make it through anything. And sometimes, once you have witnessed the lowest of the low, you can suddenly see an even higher high.

I could probably be given a free pass to deem 2021 a terrible year. My family lived in the epicenter of the global pandemic and also suffered through a horrendous car crash. But I don't see it that way at all. I see this as the year when we grew stronger, faced some of our greatest fears and moved through them and learned to keep a positive mindset throughout. We saw our friends and family rise to lift us up with love and help us through the hardest time in our lives. I believe that the lessons I have learned throughout my life allowed me to survive an incredibly difficult time and feel prepared to handle it. I am thankful for the hard times because when something unexpected happened I took it in stride. It did not define me, and it will not define me. I am stronger than that, and I know you are too.

An epilogue should signal the end, but I see this as a beginning. I want these words to give you a renewed belief that you deserve to live whatever life you choose to live, to create your life story and never look back. And I promise that I will not only write that you will be okay no matter what happens, but I will lead by example, so you can see it firsthand. To show you that if we claim our confidence there is nothing we cannot overcome, especially if we build a community of people who support each other and lift each other up.

Today is the day. Together we write our life stories and never look back.

Get out there and claim your confidence. It's time to get the life you deserve.

ACKNOWLEDGMENTS

How can I begin to thank the incredible community of people I am lucky enough to have in my life?

Mom—I couldn't do it without you. I don't know how you do everything you do: love all of us so much, give your love to so many people, and always look so put together. Thank you for everything, always. You are the gold standard of moms/mimis and I feel so lucky you are my mom. Our children are so blessed to have the magic of Mimi in their lives as well.

Dad—thank you for your never-ending stream of encouragement. It's safe to say that we all know where I inherited the ability to walk into a room full of strangers and feel energized, never scared. You are such a wonderful dad/Gunner and I love you so much.

Chris—your resilience and courage in the days after the accident showed me, once again, how lucky I am to be married to you.

Thank you for always standing by me and being my biggest supporter. Looking forward to more adventures in the coming years.

Beatrice—my amazing daughter, my travel partner. I love that you are always up for anything, filled with sunshine and positivity. I love that we share our love of music and Broadway. I hope that we can always walk around our city together sharing earbuds and belting out lyrics to musicals. I love your beautiful smile and your love of life—and I love you.

Henry—my sweet little guy. There is nothing as wonderful as the sound of your laugh. I love nothing more than cuddling up as you read books and laugh and laugh. You are such a wonderful brother to your sisters—and such a kind, loving son. I love you so much.

Eloise—my little Weezie—how you keep me on my toes. If I am eight steps ahead in the world, you are twenty. I love your sass and spunk as much as I love when you sneak into my bed at night and wake me up to tell me "I love you." I love you more. I can't wait to see what exceptional things you do in life.

Hilary—there really are no words to thank you for everything you have always done for our family, but a real gold star goes to you for the days, weeks, and months after the accident. I will never forget lying in the hospital bed with you next to me—a beacon of calm, trying hard not to make me laugh with my broken ribs (and failing miserably as you hissed like Miss Sellers) or sleeping overnight in an upright chair only to find out that it was a flat bed. You are such a wonderful aunt to the kids—I love that you meet each of them on their level and find time to spend with each of them. Thank you for being my best friend, the best travel partner in the world, and the one who never lets me keep my head in the clouds for too long.

Andrew—Pando, my always little brother. You are the rock of our family. Thank you for everything you have done for all of us over the years. The kids are lucky to have such a fun uncle in their lives, and I am lucky to have such an awesome younger brother whose apartment I use even when he doesn't know it. I'll never forget how you showed up to take care of Henry in the hospital after the accident. Love you so much.

Charles/Erin—I have never met a more perfectly matched couple. Love you both so much for your kindness, your ability to pick out the absolute perfect gift, and always being able to give the perfect recommendation for a hotel anywhere in the world. So happy that you found one another, and love you both so much.

Beth and Steve—I am so lucky to have such incredible in-laws. You have always been so generous with your time and love. Since the first day we met, you have always made me feel like I was one of your children, and I feel so lucky my children benefit from your love as much as I do. Thank you for being at the hospital that night and taking care of our kids when Chris and I couldn't. Love you both.

Katelyn—thank you for listening to each of these chapters early in the morning in the DR. Your thoughts were invaluable. Thank you for always being there for the kids and for the many, many sleepovers at your apartment! Thank you for loving our kids so much.

To my favorite British aunts—Sue, Mary, and Julia, who knew me when I was a little girl with big dreams. I have always loved the three of you so much, and remember our childhood trips to see you during the summer with such happy memories.

To Sue Garvey—thank you for always being so kind and loving to our family.

To my British cousins who live in England—so much love from across the pond. A special shout-out to Alice Kennon, who is taking over the world one day at a time. I see so much of myself in you and look forward to seeing what you conquer next! How lucky Lilla and baby Bel are to have such an incredible role model in their life.

Brooks/Ashley/Corinne and Mary—to all my "sisters" who rushed to the hospital after the accident. How blessed I am for your friendship and love. I can't tell you what it felt like to hear your voices in my room the day after the accident. To wake up to Brooks's laugh coming down the hall, see Corinne sweeping in with doughnuts with her signature giggle, or listening to Ashley, who stepped in to bring me home when I thought I might just stay in the hospital forever. You filled a dark time with so much light. You are truly angels, and I will never, ever forget what you did for my family. Love you all so much.

As always, no book or life dream will ever be complete without a shoutout to the only one whose dreams in life are as big as mine. Mary Giuliani. Quite simply, I don't know what I would do without you. You are a best friend, a soul mate, the only person who dreams as big as me. I can't wait until we finally write our children's book about the unlikely friendship between two women—one who wears high heels to a cocktail party while the other one shows up wearing muddy boots. This will be our year. Again.

Karina/Therese/Alex—I will never forget seeing your faces in the hospital. So much fear mixed with so much love. We have all been through so much since we met, and I will be forever grateful that you were all there through it all. I love all of you so much.

Mariana—you are the strongest woman I know and you will come back from all of the adversity you are facing stronger than ever before. I am so blessed to have you in my life, and I look forward to many, many years of laughter, adventures, and passport photos.

Rhea—your kindness, loving presence, and friendship mean more to me than you will ever know. You are my family always, as are your beautiful daughters. Love you.

Meg Thompson—the best agent ever. Thank you for always believing in me, approaching every situation with your calm, measured way, and caring so much about your authors. I hope this is just the beginning of our franchise!

To Jen Bergstrom and Gallery Books— simply put, I could not do any of this without your support. Thank you for everything you do to make this process so fun! Looking forward to many more books together in the future.

To Karyn Marcus—how amazing to be partnered with you on this book journey. You have taught me to dig deep and show everything, not just the good (hard as that might be!). To the *New York Times*, Times Square, and more more more!

Megan and Julia—I would never want to do this without you by my side. I am so excited that we are on this journey together. Again.

Jason Weinberg and Alex Kovacs—fifteen years later and it all starts now. Looking forward to the next chapter with Untitled.

Christine Lancman—who knew that talking could be a career?

Thank you for always supporting my dreams for the main stage. I think we might do it!

Stacy Greenberg—how can I thank you for setting everything into motion? Who could have imagined that a coffee meeting in LA would turn into a Netflix deal? You are a force, and I couldn't be more excited to be on this journey with you.

Jamie Rosengard—thank you for writing the story that started it all. I couldn't have loved our countless practice pitches and finally (!) our pitch to Netflix. To many, many more dinners at Balthazar.

To Kaitlin Dahill and Samantha Varchetto for believing in *Sold* and supporting us all the way.

To my Sewanee girls—Aubs, Lina, Brooksie, Say Say, Jamie, and Katherine—your love and support over the years has made every success sweeter and every failure a reason for laughter. You guys keep me humble while also giving me so much support. Love you all.

Scottie—so proud of you for everything you are doing. Keep going—the sky is the limit.

Kate Schelter—for my daily texts post-accident and your friendship over the years. I love you and can't wait to see your brand vision come to life. To Soho and beyond!

Cena, Alex, and Sara—I'll never forget our NYC adventures in 2020 and 2021. Here's to more laughter always.

Amory—my boss lawyer for negotiating everything and magnums of champagne.

Geoff and Heidi—love the six of you like family. We are so lucky to have you in our lives and look forward to many more fun adventures in the future as Heidi builds her empire!

Rob and Erin—love you for friendship always. So blessed to have you in our lives.

Cailtin and Mick Davis—for too many fun nights with side-splitting laughter in Greenwich to count, and many more to come.

Lexy/Lily/Suus/Kseniia/Poppy/Benny/Stella—how I loved every laugh, cry, and everything in between during our Strat Par years. How lucky was I to get to spend my days with you. I hope you follow your path and get everything you want out of life. I am rooting for you every step of the way.

Courtney—my networking breakfast partner. Through all the ups and downs you continue to live life with such joy. Your energy and spirit are infectious.

Polly from Capetown—to many more nights out in foreign countries having adventures that border on sketchy but always make for a good story. Cap Estel will always be our benchmark.

Mallory Page and Jacques Rodrigue—my Cajun sages. How I love spending time back down in Louisiana with you. To many more rides on Lake Pontchartrain.

Cheri, Whitney, Libba, Jackie, and Ladies of the Southern C— thank you for putting together the most amazing forum for women ever and making the first week of February my favorite week of the year.

A shoutout to my friends who inspire me every day—John McCann, Beth McCann, Lindsey Goldfaden, Jeff Goldfaden, Tom Menacho, Grant Frankel, Henrik Lundqvist, John Heffers, Brian Haklisch, Amy Haklisch, Brooke Pederson, Miriam Shaw, Lauren Mulholland, Jocelyn Gailliot, Jenna Hager, Henry Hager, Henry Johnson, Laird

Gough, Savannah Guthrie, Michelle Choo, Tanaz Eshaghian, Mary Cannon, Brooke Monahan, Phoebe Polk, Bergin O'Malley, Liz Hallock, Laurent Claquin, Jamie and Jackie Dimitri, Josh Holdeman, Sara Rugova, Rachelle MacPherson, Grady and Amanda Frank, Lauren Netter, Molly Fienning, Stacy Smallwood, Ashley Miles, Martine Chaisson, Keith Fox, Daniel Lurie, Becca Prowda, Andrea Fiuczynski, Brandon Shorenstein, Danielle Snyder, Brett and Morgan Hutchinson, Jenny Rothenberg, Adam and Andrea Saper, Marlaine Olinick, Ben and Lizzie Leventhal, Lauren Nanna, Josh Wood, Mimi Eayrs, Davin Staats, Agatha Capacchione, and Ryan Hardy.

A huge shout-out to the Grace Church community that rallied around us with so much love and support after the accident.

To my ride or die Christie's OG—Lauren Land, Nikole Yurt, and Sydney Blumenkranz. So proud to see the three of you continuing to rock the world as you have since our early days in special events.

To Lauren Shortt for showing me what empathy and kindness look like in leadership. You taught me at a young age what it looks like to run a team with grace and kindness. To George McNeely, who will always be my favorite dance partner.

To the amazing contributors—Ashley Baker, Trish McEvoy, Ruchi Kotahwala, Maggie Smith, Allison Wyatt, Cheri Levy, Whitney Long, Eve Rodsky, Stephanie Hall, Beatrice Dixon, Meena Flynn, Zibby Owens, and Rachelle Hruska. Thank you for the gift of your words. I know so many women will benefit from reading them.

To Marc Porter, Maria Los, Jonathan Rendell, Stephen Lash, Bonnie Brennan, Jen Hall, Sheri Farber, Gemma Sudlow, Lolita Persaud, Stacy Sayer, Sam Margolis, Devang Thakkar, Michael Moore, Cathy Busch, Ellanor Notides, Tash Perrin, Ben Whine, Capera Ryan, Jessica Katz, Allison Whiting, Matt Rubinger, Lillian Vasquez, James Gandia, Jen Zatorski, Ellen Berkley, Alexandra Reid, and countless others I have worked with for your support and friendship over so many years.

To Daniella—who pulled over on the side of the road the night of the accident and protected my children. I will never forget your kindness as long as I live.

A shout-out to the Apawamis community—my tennis crew in particular—who rallied around us after the accident.

How can I ever truly thank the medical team at Westchester Medical Center for taking care of my family on that fateful Halloween night. Your kindness, patience, and care will never be forgotten. A special thank-you to all of the nurses who watched over me—and the nurses who watched over my children. In particular, Chelsea, who carried Beatrice on her back to the bathroom every night while she stayed in the hospital. The biggest shout-out goes to Dr. Merritt Kinon, who fused my spine back together and created a scar I will proudly wear for the rest of my life. I will never forget how patiently you sat next to my bed listening to our questions. You will forever be known as Dr. Phenomenal in our family!

Finally, a huge thank-you to all my readers for your support. I love hearing from each and every one of you, so keep emailing, sending messages, and connecting on social. Your words and stories inspire me to keep writing. I couldn't do it without you.

158.1 FEN

Fenet, Lydia
Claim your confidence
: unlock your

04/07/23